Life in the Land of the Pharaohs

JOURNEYS INTO THE PAST

LIFE IN THE LAND OF THE PHARAOHS

Published by
THE READER'S DIGEST ASSOCIATION LIMITED
LONDON NEW YORK SYDNEY MONTREAL CAPE TOWN

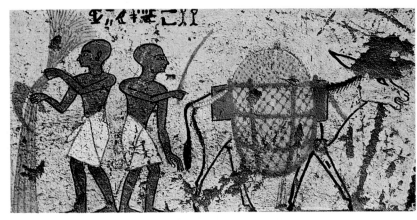

PEASANT LIFE Egyptian society was fed by field workers like these, depicted in a tomb scene from ancient Thebes.

FAMILY VALUES Marriage was the central institution of everyday life.

LIFE IN THE LAND OF THE PHARAOHS
Edited and designed by Toucan Books Limited
Sole author: Tim Healey

First edition copyright © 1995
The Reader's Digest Association Limited,
11 Westferry Circus, Canary Wharf, London E14 4HE

Reprinted 1999

Copyright © 1995
Reader's Digest Association Far East Limited
Philippines copyright © 1995
Reader's Digest Association Far East Limited

Printing and binding: Printer Industria Gráfica S.A., Barcelona
Separations: Typongraph, Verona, Italy
Paper: Perigord-Condat, France

ISBN 0 276 42123 X

Page 1: Model of an Egyptian ship from the Middle Kingdom period.
Pages 2-3: Servants bring provisions to sustain an official in the afterlife.
Front cover (clockwise from top left): Harvest god, Amun; funerary papyrus of a royal scribe Hunefer; scarab pectoral from tomb of Tutankhamun, Thebes; priest Teuti and his wife; sphinx and pyramid, Giza; donkey and peasants.
Back cover: Scribe and monkey-god Thoth; wall paintings from tomb of Sennefer, Thebes; fly-whisk from tomb of Tutankhamun; cosmetic spoon.

PENMANSHIP Thoth, god of learning, watches a scribe at work. Administration called for officials who could read and write.

CALL TO ARMS The ranks of Egyptian soldiery were swelled by Nubian and other foreign mercenaries.

COSMETIC SPOON Wealthy Egyptians were no strangers to life's little vanities.

CONTENTS

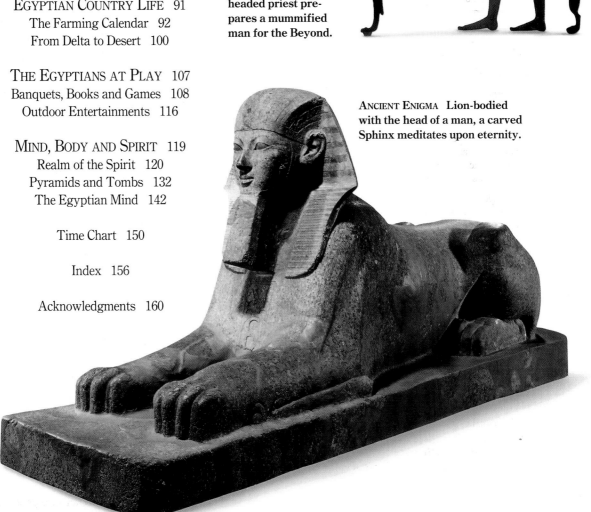

THE AFTERLIFE Mourners grieved noisily at funerals, but for the Egyptians death was not the end. Right: a jackal-headed priest prepares a mummified man for the Beyond.

ANCIENT ENIGMA Lion-bodied with the head of a man, a carved Sphinx meditates upon eternity.

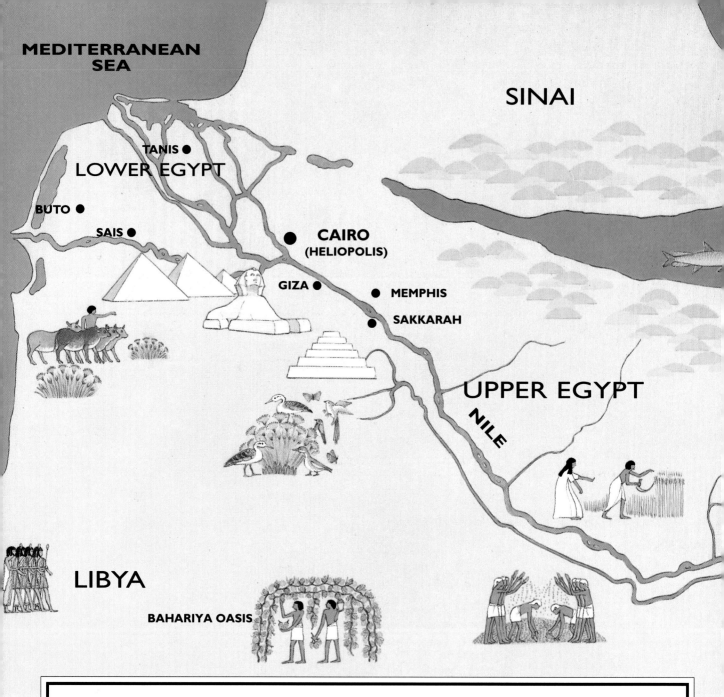

MEDITERRANEAN
SEA

SINAI

TANIS ●
LOWER EGYPT

BUTO ●

SAIS ●

CAIRO
(HELIOPOLIS)

GIZA ●

MEMPHIS ●

SAKKARAH ●

UPPER EGYPT

NILE

LIBYA

BAHARIYA OASIS

THE LIFE-GIVING NILE

FOR MUCH of Egypt's history, road transport barely existed. Most of the country's traffic was by ship along the Nile which, besides nourishing the land, became the main thoroughfare.

The Nile also gave Egypt its unity and form. The granite barrier of the Cataract at Aswan marked a natural southern frontier. Flowing north, the river cut a valley through the sandstone and limestone plateau, until it reached the sea. Over thousands of years the Nile deposited an ever deeper layer of silt as it neared the sea, creating the Delta. The river ran through the Delta in seven main branches, before dividing into many smaller streams.

This land, Lower Egypt, was marshy and studded with lagoons; but it also contained rich agricultural land. This is why the central delta has been one of the most densely populated parts of the country throughout Egypt's history. From the earliest times, the region was united as one kingdom under the protection of the cobra goddess, and its king wore the Red Crown.

Upper Egypt stretched along the river valley as far as Aswan. Its patron was the vulture goddess of Nekheb, whose kings wore the White Crown. When the kings of Upper Egypt conquered Lower Egypt, in about 3100 BC, they united the two crowns, and built a new capital at Memphis.

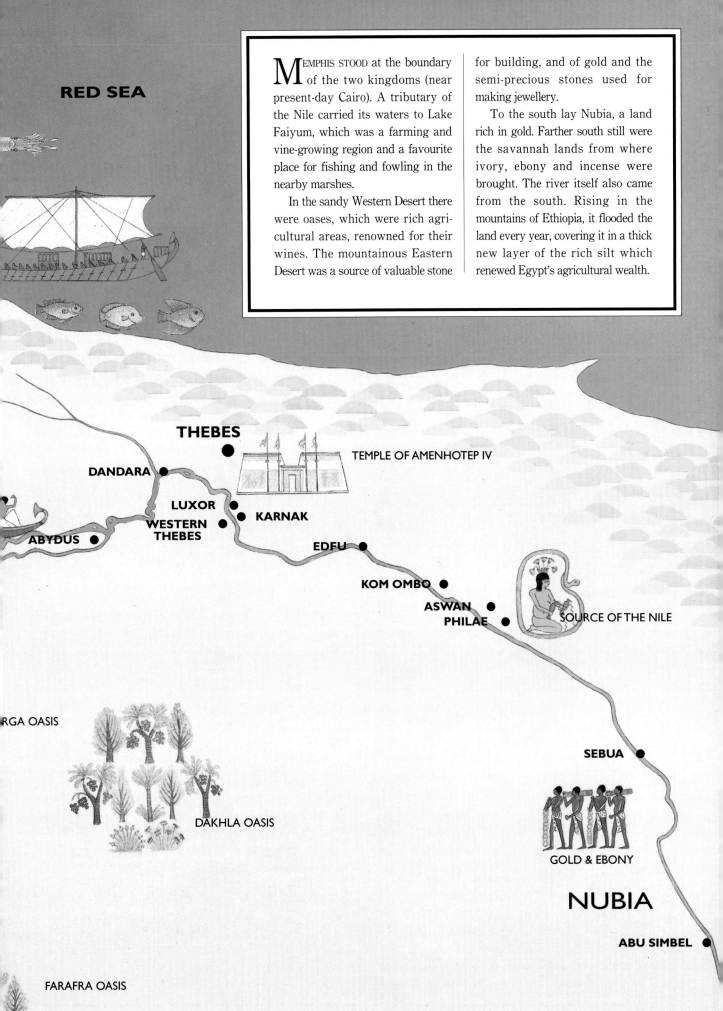

RED SEA

MEMPHIS STOOD at the boundary of the two kingdoms (near present-day Cairo). A tributary of the Nile carried its waters to Lake Faiyum, which was a farming and vine-growing region and a favourite place for fishing and fowling in the nearby marshes.

In the sandy Western Desert there were oases, which were rich agricultural areas, renowned for their wines. The mountainous Eastern Desert was a source of valuable stone for building, and of gold and the semi-precious stones used for making jewellery.

To the south lay Nubia, a land rich in gold. Farther south still were the savannah lands from where ivory, ebony and incense were brought. The river itself also came from the south. Rising in the mountains of Ethiopia, it flooded the land every year, covering it in a thick new layer of the rich silt which renewed Egypt's agricultural wealth.

THEBES

TEMPLE OF AMENHOTEP IV

DANDARA

LUXOR

KARNAK

WESTERN THEBES

ABYDUS

EDFU

KOM OMBO

ASWAN

PHILAE

SOURCE OF THE NILE

RGA OASIS

DAKHLA OASIS

SEBUA

GOLD & EBONY

NUBIA

FARAFRA OASIS

ABU SIMBEL

WHO WERE THE EGYPTIANS?

Alongside the great desert waterway of the Nile there grew a glittering civilisation ruled by

an elite of star-gazing priests, literate and leisured nobles, learned scribes –

and kings who thought themselves living gods.

O MANY PEOPLE, the realm of the pharaohs is a place of compelling mystery. In the land of the Sphinx lay the splendours of the great pyramids, the monumental temples of Karnak and Luxor, and the hidden tombs of the Valley of the Kings. It was a land, too, of strange gods – Isis, Osiris and Anubis, the jackal-headed god of ritual embalmment. Stories about a supposed Curse of Tutankhamun and horror films about tomb terrors have enhanced the idea that ancient Egypt was a place of dark enigma. Was it really so mysterious? Who were the ancient Egyptians? And how did they build their advanced civilisation?

It is now known that nomadic hunters were roaming the banks of the Nile throughout the Stone Age period, and that by about 7000 BC they were making seasonal campsites to take advantage of the river's good fishing. From about 6000 BC people were starting to farm and to herd at permanent settlements, planting emmer wheat and barley, and growing flax to make linen. Vast riverside thickets of reeds, rushes and coarse grasses furnished material for skilfully woven mats and baskets, while the Nile mud provided clay for pottery. And already the first Egyptians were revealing how much religion meant to them. For in the places where they buried their dead, they also buried cows, jackals and sheep, wrapped in shrouds.

THE THIN LAND

The people's destiny was shaped by one of the world's mightiest rivers. Flowing 750 miles from the great cataract near present-day Aswan to its delta on the Mediterranean, the Nile ploughed a long, lush furrow through the desert. Egypt was a thin ribbon of land, extending at most a few miles on one or other side of the river. But it was immensely fertile. Every year the river flooded its banks to nourish the land with a fresh deposit of rich silt. Once the people had learned the basics of flood management, the rewards were immense. Bumper crops freed members of the community from farmwork to devote themselves to specialist tasks. Surplus grain fed a wealth of craftsmen who never needed to enter the fields: carpenters, goldsmiths, stonemasons, weavers, sculptors, jewellers and many others. It was out of this widening cast of characters that town life evolved in Egypt.

Urban society started to take shape in about 3500 BC and, cradled by the desert, Egypt was self-sufficient in most respects. Except for timber, craftsmen had all the essential raw materials at hand. Good-sized logs, however, had to be imported by sea from the Lebanon, and the Egyptians also developed an early desire for luxury items. They imported silver and lapis lazuli from western Asia, for example. From a land they called Punt, somewhere on the coast of modern Ethiopia, and from Kush (northern Sudan), they obtained incense, ivory, sandalwood and exotic animals such as giraffes, monkeys and baboons. Trade with the sophisticated people of Elam (south-west Iran) and Mesopotamia must have triggered new

FOREIGN CAPTIVES The images depict Egypt's Libyan, Nubian, Asiatic, Syrian and Hittite neighbours.

ideas. For the Egyptians were by no means the only pioneers of civilisation. The skills of writing, metalworking and building with mud bricks were practised in Mesopotamia before Egypt. And the two burgeoning civilisations are known to have been in some sort of contact with one another, either by sea around the Arabian peninsula, or by donkey caravans along the long, dusty trails leading through Syria and Palestine.

Doing business with the lively Mesopotamians may have stimulated the Nile's people. Yet the Egyptians created such a distinctive culture that foreign influence cannot explain it. They were essentially isolated from the rest of the world, and happy with that state of affairs. What grew up along the Nile was a civilisation wedded to its own landscape. Not only did the Nile irrigate and fertilise the country, it also served as the main highway connecting the two contrasting regions of Upper Egypt and Lower Egypt. It was when these two different regions were united under one political authority that the age of the pharaohs dawned.

THE COMING OF THE PHARAOHS
Early Egypt's political history is a jigsaw puzzle from which most of the pieces are missing. Nevertheless, it is known that from about 3500 to 3100 BC sizable towns were growing up along the Nile valley. At Naqada and Hierakonpolis in Upper Egypt excavated tombs

THE RIVER PEOPLE Fishermen hunt among the papyrus beds. The Nile shaped Egypt's destiny.

FIRST PHARAOH The mighty Narmer, thought to have been Egypt's first king, marches in triumphal procession.

also show, through their differences in size, that a real gap was opening between the status of different members of society. Relics recovered from these sites depict images of power and strife, and the towns themselves were walled – clearly a defensive measure. Everything suggests a society of warring kingdoms, centred on the main urban areas.

Then came a momentous event. Around 3100 BC, Upper and Lower Egypt were united by the first pharaoh, a legendary figure called Menes. He is named as founder of the 1st dynasty in a history of Egypt written in the 3rd century BC, and seems to have been the same man as a pharaoh called Narmer whose picture appears on ceremonial artefacts from

YEARS

3000	2900	2800	2700	2600	2500	2400	2300	2200	2100	2000	1900	1800	1700	1600	1500

| | OLD KINGDOM 2686-2181 BC | MIDDLE KINGDOM 2033-1650 BC | |

| Pre dynastic: before 3150 BC | Early Dynastic Period: 3150-2686 BC | First Inter- mediate Period: 2134- 2023 BC | Second In- termediate Period: 1660- 1570 BC |

1st dynasty 3050-2890 BC	3rd dynasty 2681-2613 BC	9th dynasty	11th dynasty	14th dynasty ?	18th
2nd dynasty 2890-2686 BC	4th dynasty 2613-2498 BC	2160-2130 BC	2033-1973 BC	15th dynasty	19th
	5th dynasty 2498-2345 BC	10th dynasty	12th dynasty	1660-1155 BC	20th
	6th dynasty 2345-2181 BC	2130-2033 BC	1973-1797 BC	16th dynasty ?	
	7th dynasty 2181 BC-?	11th dynasty	13th dynasty	17th dynasty	
	8th dynasty ?-2160 BC	2133-2033 BC	1796-1660 BC	1660-1570 BC	

• Narmer   • Djoser   • Pepy   • Menthuhotep • Senusret   • Hyksos • Ahmose

• Khufu   • Amenemhat   • Hatshe

• Akhen

Tutan

UNDERLINGS Egypt was a master-and-servant society. Here, bearers bring offerings to their lord.

Hierakonpolis. Narmer was a mighty conqueror: he is shown on a macehead enthroned under the image of a vulture goddess, with his fan-bearers and sandal-bearers in attendance, with captives numbering 120 000 men, 400 000 cattle and 1 422 000 goats, and a lady being carried in a litter – perhaps a captured princess. As evidence that he was indeed master of the Two Lands, Narmer wears the double crown. Combining the red crown of Lower Egypt with the white crown of Upper Egypt, this would remain the symbol of the pharaoh through ages to come.

Thirty dynasties of pharaohs followed after the unification, independence ending with the absorption of Egypt into the Roman Empire in 30 BC. For well over 3000 years Egyptian society was to evolve, through periods of pyramid-building, eras of expansion and times of unrest, always with an amazing underlying continuity. The vast deserts around Egypt sheltered her from all but the most determined enemies. For generation upon generation the life-giving Nile continued to nourish the people. And – except for relatively brief (*continued on p.15*)

(*continued on p.15*)

									YEARS AD		
1200	1100	1000	900	800	700	600	500	400	300	200	100	0	100	200	300

OM

Third Intermediate Period: 1070-656 BC	Late Dynastic Period: 664-332 BC	Greek Period: 332-30 BC	Roman Period: 30 BC-AD 323

0-1293 BC	21st dynasty 1069-945 BC	26th dynasty 664-525 BC	Macedonian
3-1185 BC	22nd dynasty 945-700 BC	27th dynasty 525-404 BC	and
5-1070 BC	23rd dynasty	28th dynasty 404-399 BC	Ptolemaic
	24th dynasty	29th dynasty 399-380 BC	Dynasties
	25th dynasty 710-656 BC	30th dynasty 380-342 BC	

| mses II | • Libyan kings and Kushite kings | • Persian Empire | • Alexander the Great | • Ptolemy |
| | | | | • Cleopatra |

11

RECONSTRUCTING THE PAST

Roman historians, Old Master painters and pioneer archaeologists have all helped to shape modern perceptions about Egypt.

BEFORE the development of archaeology as we know it today, there were two main sources of information about ancient Egypt available to European scholars. The first of these was the Bible in which Egypt figured prominently, notably in the stories of Joseph and the Exodus in the Old Testament, and in the New Testament as the refuge of the Holy Family. The other great tradition was that of the Greek and Roman writers, such as Herodotus, whose works had been preserved throughout the medieval period and had been a major inspiration to the artists and architects of the Renaissance.

These fragments of Egypt's history included the conflict between Egypt under its last rulers, the Ptolemaic dynasty, and the rising power of Rome – and provided what was to become one of the world's greatest love stories, that of the Roman General Mark Antony and the Egyptian queen, Cleopatra.

The defeat of their combined fleet at the Battle of Actium in 30 BC, and the suicide of Cleopatra the following

EGYPT IN ROME Statue of Hadrian's favourite, Antinous, in the kilt and headcloth of a pharaoh.

year, brought Egypt into the Roman Empire. It also led to the removal of many obelisks, statues and other massive stone monuments from Egypt to adorn the city of Rome. In fact, there are more obelisks in Rome today than there are still standing in Egypt itself.

Egyptian religion, particularly the worship of the goddess Isis, spread throughout the Roman world, and influenced the imagery of early Christianity. In the 2nd century AD

NILE QUEEN The life and loves of Cleopatra have inspired western artists.

the Roman emperor, Hadrian, developed a special attachment to Egypt. As he was touring the country, his favourite, Antinous, was drowned in the Nile. The grief-stricken emperor proclaimed him a god, and the youth was shown wearing the kilt and headcloth of the pharaohs, although the style of the statues was typically classical. Back in Italy, Hadrian adorned his enormous villa at Tivoli outside Rome with statues of Antinous, and with monuments removed from Egypt.

In the centuries following the

conquest of Egypt by the Arabs in AD 670, there was considerably less contact with western Europe, but the Biblical and classical traditions ensured Egypt a place in the western consciousness. The Renaissance led to a renewal of interest, which was stimulated further during the papal rebuilding of Rome during the 16th century when many of the Egyptian monuments that had been taken to the city by the Romans were uncovered. There was another burst of interest in the ancient world in the 18th century when much of the sculpture that had adorned Hadrian's villa at Tivoli was found.

But it was not until the French military expedition led by Napoleon in 1798 that Egypt itself was opened to Europeans. Napoleon's expedition included many scholars, and in the decades that followed similar expeditions were sent by other European powers to record the monuments. The French had assembled a collection of antiquities that was due to be taken to Paris, but this was captured by the British. The collection included the inscribed block now known as the 'Rosetta stone', which provided the key to the decipherment of hieroglyphics in the 1820s.

The antiquities race was on. One

IMPERIAL EXPLORERS The Lepsius expedition on top of the Great Pyramid.

of the most significant European expeditions was that sent by Prussia, and led by Karl-Richard Lepsius. Between 1842 and 1845 the expedition covered the whole of the Nile valley from the Delta far into Sudan, copying temple and tomb scenes and inscriptions. The world's knowledge of ancient Egypt expanded rapidly.

The pillage of the monuments that had marked the early years of the 19th century was gradually replaced by a greater concern with preservation and interest in objects of daily life rather than big monuments. Modern archaeology began in the last years of the 19th century, and has become increasingly scientific. Spectacular finds, such as the tomb of Tutankhamun by the British archaeologist Howard Carter in November 1922, produced a dazzling array of art objects, but told us less about the daily life of the ordinary people of Ancient Egypt than the excavation, for example, of humble mud-brick villages.

TUTANKHAMUN Carter spent ten years clearing the tomb.

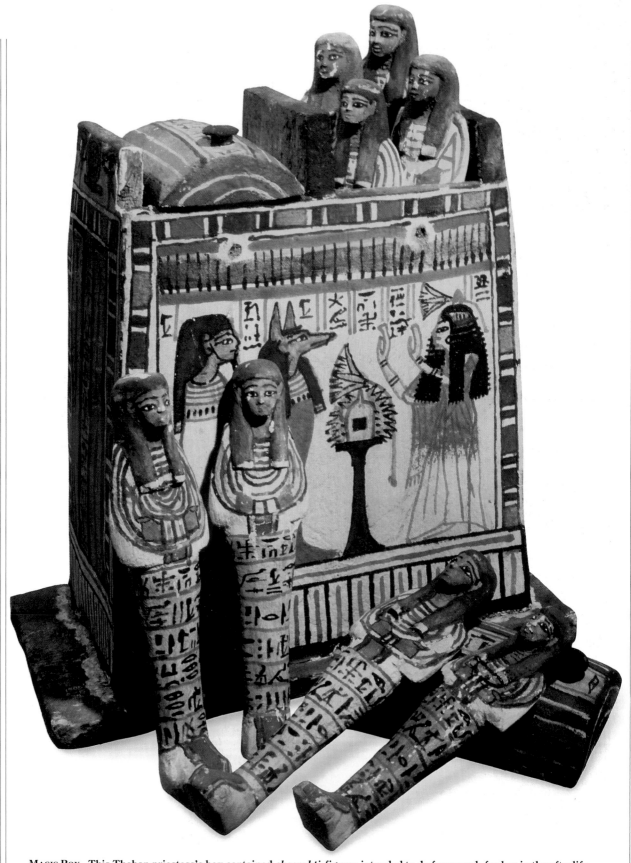

MAGIC BOX This Theban priestess's box contained *shawabti* figures intended to do farm work for her in the afterlife.

interludes of foreign domination and civil disorder – the pharaoh remained undisputed ruler, presiding over all with the majesty of a god.

The word pharaoh derives from the Egyptian words for 'Great House'. Pronounced something like *per a'o*, the title implies a particular respect for the ruler, as if it would be impertinent to refer to him by name. For the pharaoh was thought of as a semi-divine being, acting as an intermediary between heaven and earth. Bound around his brow was the royal cobra, symbol of the sun god Re. And when enthroned in full regalia he appeared as the incarnation of the falcon deity Horus. The pharaoh's power was absolute – he existed to be obeyed.

THE AURA OF MAGIC

Lit with divinity, the pharaoh stood at the very top of a pyramid-like society. Down through its widening base, religion and magic penetrated every layer of the civilisation in a way that modern Westerners cannot easily understand. The class of scribes, or literate officials, acted as the pharaoh's administrators. But the servants of the state were also servants of a godlike figure, so there was no clear distinction between bureaucracy and religion. Whether seeking the cause of a natural catastrophe or a minor human ailment, the ancient Egyptians looked for an explanation in the agency of unseen gods. Magic and medicine were one. Egyptian doctors were respected throughout the ancient world, yet despite their attempts to categorise diseases and systematise treatment, they called continually on supernatural powers through magical incantations and spells.

Forms of expression in ancient Egyptian documents sometimes sound so strange to the modern ear that it becomes easy to imagine a people more awestruck and haunted by superstition than may have been the case. Egypt was, after all, an authoritarian state which, like others throughout history, churned out propaganda to suit its own purposes. State officials, doctors and priests all had their own reasons for creating mystique, and the real beliefs of ordinary men and women are not easy to gauge. Did the priests' sacred rituals and the doctors' incantations seem like so much mumbo-jumbo to the average peasant? Perhaps this was sometimes so. But there is ample evidence that magic and religion permeated all levels of society. Charms and amulets,

WORKING PEOPLE Humble fishermen operate a dragnet on the bountiful waters of the Nile.

designed to ward off hostile forces, abound among the relics of Egyptians from every social class. Household shrines have been found in the homes of artisans as well as nobles, and prayers have endured that were uttered not only by priests but also by working men.

The problem is that the private thoughts of the poor were rarely committed to writing, and their homes were made of perishable materials. What have survived are Egypt's great stone-built monuments – temples and pyramids – as well as brightly coloured wall paintings, coffins and household treasures from the tombs of the privileged classes.

The survival of the tombs accounts more than anything else for Egypt's reputation as a death-orientated society. There is no escaping the fact that the Egyptians were, as a people, unusually preoccupied with the Beyond. Yet what the tomb paintings and furnishings also depict is a people who loved life and colour. When they painted the teeming wildlife of the Nile they depicted minutely observed species of animals, fish, butterflies and birds. Ducks, geese, storks, herons and kingfishers are all represented with such accurate detail that they might serve in a modern birdwatcher's handbook. Here are images of people at work and at play: harvesting crops, tending their vines, holding dinner parties, drinking and dancing to the music of lute, oboe and tambourine.

Tomb relics show that Egyptian families kept pets. Board games and children's toys have survived, including whip tops, rag dolls, and puppets whose limbs twitched into life when strings were pulled. Egypt boasted wine connoisseurs and a fashion-conscious nobility with elaborate wigs, fragrant perfumes, shaving razors, eye-paint pots and cosmetic creams. Luxury glassware, fine jewellery and elegant furniture inlaid with ebony and ivory . . . all speak of a worldly people who knew how to enjoy themselves – if they had the wealth and leisure to do so.

For the great mass of the people, no doubt, life was hard. Among the few working people's homes that have been excavated, archaeologists have come upon some very cramped, terraced dwellings whose inhabitants must have endured joyless, regimented lives. But there were skilled workers who lived more comfortably, and were no strangers to life's luxuries. The epic film-makers' notion of Egypt as a society of the ant-heap, with worker-slaves dehumanised by their all-powerful ruler, seems misleading to modern scholars. The Egyptians were a people of flesh and blood, with everyday problems and normal human concerns. In fact, the very ordinariness of life 4000 years ago is as fascinating in its way as Egypt's exotic character. The truth is that people bore children, wrote letters, took baths, negotiated business deals, got drunk, fell in love, worried about their families, gossiped and grumbled about their wages – all in the shadow of the towering pyramids, and of the god-king known as the pharaoh.

CORNUCOPIA The Nile valley yielded grapes, wildfowl and sweetmeats for those with the wealth to enjoy them.

LIFE IN THE EGYPTIAN FAMILY

The Egyptians were preoccupied – as other peoples have been throughout history –
with everyday family matters. The scene from Amarna above shows the pharaoh
Akhenaten and his wife Nefertiti playing with three of their children. In town and
country alike, people concerned themselves with the age-old problems of seeking a
marriage partner, choosing names for their babies and sorting out questions
of wills and inheritance.

COURTSHIP, LOVE AND MARRIAGE

'Follow your heart as long as you live!' was the maxim of one

Middle Kingdom sage. The Egyptians commended spontaneous emotion,

and honoured love between men and women.

HUSBANDS AND WIVES often appear in Egyptian sculpture sitting side by side and holding hands in obvious gestures of affection. They look easy in one another's company, almost like modern couples posing for the family album. This kind of bonding between men and women is rarely shown in the art of other ancient civilisations, but in Egypt, marriage was the central institution of social life and contained elements of true partnership.

There was, however, no formal marriage ceremony – not even a word for wedding. The Egyptian expression for marriage was 'founding a house', and a couple sealed their relationship simply by setting up home together. Though it is reasonable to assume that families sometimes threw big parties to celebrate the union, there is no evidence for it. In fact, the only formalities involved were legal agreements drawn up privately between the two sides to establish rights concerning maintenance and the couple's possessions. The fascinating thing about these documents is the extent of women's property rights compared to

LOVING COUPLE Hand in hand, an Egyptian husband and wife stride together down the road of life.

other societies of the time. As long as the marriage lasted, the wife remained the owner of what she had brought into the household. In the event of divorce, she generally received a third of the assets acquired during the marriage, and was also entitled to maintenance. Even a woman who had been divorced on grounds of adultery retained certain rights to maintenance from her former partner.

If one marriage partner simply did not get on with the other, that was considered sufficient grounds for divorce. Wanting to marry someone else was also regarded as a perfectly adequate reason for separation. As men rose higher in the ranks of officialdom, they might sometimes reject a first wife solely in order to pair up with a woman of higher standing. In one letter addressed by a grieving Egyptian to his dead wife, the writer congratulates himself on doing no such thing: 'I was with you when I was carrying out all sorts of offices. I was with you and I did not divorce you. I did not cause your heart to grieve. I did it when I was a youth and when I was carrying out all sorts of important offices for the Pharaoh, [to whom be all] life, prosperity, health, without divorcing you, saying "She has always been with me – so said I!" '

Divorce itself was easily obtained. Either partner could simply renounce the other, with or without their consent. One of them would then leave home. A husband's obligations to support his former wife must have caused many men to pause for thought before trying to rid himself of his partner. None the less, divorce was far from rare in ancient Egypt and priests made no effort to hold couples together. Marriage, it seems, was not considered to be a sacred institution.

Written agreements between couples were, of course, confined to the upper classes. Little is known about marriage arrangements among the great mass of peasants and workmen, but it is likely that vows were made at the time when a couple set up home. This is certainly suggested by

TOGETHERNESS A harpist plays to entertain an Egyptian couple. Below: a marriage document dating from 172 BC. In it, the groom agrees to pay the bride a given sum within 30 days should the marriage end in divorce.

a broken piece of limestone recovered from Deir el-Medina. Dating back to the reign of Ramses III (1182-1151 BC) it carries a unique inscription proclaiming that on a particular day a workman called Telmont came before a scribe and foreman saying, 'Let Nekhemmut swear an oath to the Lord that he will not desert my daughter.' Nekhemmut's oath follows: 'As Amun lives and the Ruler lives! If I ever desert the daughter of Telmont, I will be liable to a hundred lashes and I will lose all that I have acquired together with her.'

The terms of this oath seem exceptionally severe. All the same, it is obvious that where pressure was applied to keep a marriage going, it was more likely to come from concerned parents than from any lawyer or priest. In a letter to his daughter a father from Deir el-Medina promises:

TENDER TOUCH A scene from the back of Tutankhamun's gold throne shows the young pharaoh being anointed with oil by his queen.

19

A BEARDED WOMAN

Queen Hatshepsut (*c.*1490-1468 BC) was the first woman pharaoh, and to fulfil her role she had to assume all the masculine trappings of kingship. Statues show her in men's clothing. Sometimes she is even depicted wearing the traditional false beard of the pharaoh – a goatee that had been worn for ritualistic reasons since ancient times.

'If the workman Baki throws you out of the house, I will take action!' As for alternative accommodation: 'You may dwell in the anteroom to my storehouse because it is I who built it. Nobody in the world shall throw you out of there.'

Egyptian girls often married young – the age of 14 seems to have been not unusual. For men, the age of 20 was recommended in the teachings of one scribe, while another suggested: 'Take a wife while you are young, so that she may make a son for you. She should bear for you while you are youthful.' Parents arranged many marriages for their offspring, and because Egypt had an extremely strict social structure, partners were normally found within an individual's own social class. In fact, marriages within the family – between first cousins, for example – were not unknown.

ROYAL INCEST

Marriages between brother and sister also occurred, at least within the royal household: the founder of the 18th dynasty, Ahmose (*c.*1570-1546 BC), for example,

HEARTH AND HOME Marriage meant 'founding a house' – often a square-built dwelling of modest size. A column supported the ceiling in the main room. Awnings on roof and in the courtyard provided additional living space.

DO THE PAINTINGS LIE?

ALMOND-EYED BEAUTIES in skin-tight sheath dresses . . . broad-shouldered men with narrow waists and flat stomachs . . . smiling peasants and dutiful servants . . . the tomb paintings of ancient Egypt present an attractive picture of an orderly world inhabited by a healthy, happy people. But do the paintings tell the truth?

Egyptian art served a sacred function in society, and basically idealised its subject matter. The temples and tombs were the realms of the gods and of the departed: from their precincts, all hints of sickness or deformity were banished. No one in the tomb paintings suffers from middle-age spread. Old age is not depicted – everyone is represented as young and slender, so that it is hard to tell a father from his son, a mother from her daughter, without the aid of hieroglyphic captions.

Age-old conventions dictated how things should appear, and although individual images might be minutely detailed, the artists' first concern was not to paint what they saw. It was to engineer magic – to provide the departed with resources for the afterlife. Ancient tradition decided that human figures should be drawn in profile, but with one eye and both shoulders seen frontally. And the tomb owner should always be the largest figure, not because he was the tallest, but because he was the most important. It was not the artists' place to question such traditions.

The paintings may not exactly lie, but they have certainly led to a few misunderstandings. Some of the figure-hugging sheath dresses of the women, for example, can never have been worn in real life. They would have been impossible to walk in, and were obviously painted – to show off the shapeliness of the female form. Real dresses discovered from the Egyptian period are noticeably

SKIN TIGHT Artists and sculptors depicted women in garments that fitted too close for comfort.

baggier. Additionally, tradition urged that a man's body be shown as a dark, reddish-brown and a woman's a lighter, yellowish-brown, probably symbolising the fact that men generally worked out of doors while women remained largely indoors.

Altogether, Egyptian paintings provide a wealth of fascinating information about life under the pharaohs – but it is information to be interpreted with care. Quirkier, more candid glimpses of life are supplied by Egypt's painted 'ostraca' (from the Greek word *ostrakon* meaning 'potsherd'). These were simple flakes of white limestone used much like jotting pads, and on them artists often did sketches and comic doodles with a refreshing irreverence. Many ostraca scenes involve animals dolled up to look like humans: a cat holding a fan and napkin presents a roasted goose to a pompous-looking rat; a lady mouse parades herself in fine pleated garments; an army of mice force the surrender of cats in their fortress. The intention is often clearly satirical, and the tomb scenes suggest a healthy undercurrent of subversive humour among the ordinary working people.

COMIC RELIEF Artists' doodles on limestone fragments display a puckish humour absent from most of Egypt's official paintings.

certainly wedded his sister Ahmose-Nofretari. In other cases, monarchs took half-sisters as their spouses – and had children by them. Some kings even married their daughters. The reason for these incestuous relationships is not precisely known, but for a long time scholars explained them with the notion that the right to Egypt's throne was determined by marriage with the 'heiress' – the daughter of the previous queen. This, it was said, ensured the legitimacy of the line. In reality, no such line of descent can be traced in Egyptian history – there are simply too many pharaohs who had wives of non-royal origin to support the 'heiress' theory. Marriage within the family seems rather to have reflected the fact that the pharaohs were regarded, and regarded themselves, as gods. The sun god, whose mother became his wife, who became his daughter, provided an image of perpetual regeneration.

Marriages between brothers and sisters were, however, rare even in the royal household, and the words 'brother' and 'sister' which often appear in love poems were terms of endearment. A number of romantic lyrics have survived from ancient Egypt, and their torrid tone demonstrates that even if some marriages were fixed by the parents, there were many courting couples who shared intense feelings for one another. In this New Kingdom lyric, for example, a lovelorn young man yearns for a girl he has not seen for several days:

> *Seven days to yesterday I have not seen the sister,*
> *And a sickness has invaded me.*
> *My body has become heavy,*
> *Forgetful of my own self.*
> *If the chief of physicians comes to me*
> *My heart is not content with his remedies . . .*

DIVINE UNION **The pharaohs believed that they enjoyed a special relationship with the gods. Here, Sety I communes with the love goddess Hathor.**

ANCIENT LOVE LYRICS

THE LOVE POEMS written during the New Kingdom are richly sensual:

> *She looks like the rising morning star*
> *At the start of a happy year.*
> *Shining bright, fair of skin,*
> *Lovely the look of her eyes,*
> *Sweet the speech of her lips,*

> *She has not a word too much.*
> *Upright neck, shining breast*
> *Hair true lapis lazuli;*
> *Arms surpassing gold,*
> *Fingers like lotus buds.*

> *Heavy thighs, narrow waist,*
> *Her legs parade her beauty;*
> *With graceful step she treads the ground,*
> *Captures my heart by her movements.*

From a papyrus dating from the reign of Ramses V c.1145 BC

Girls longed for their male lovers with similar ardour:

My brother torments my heart with his voice,
He makes sickness take hold of me;
He is neighbour to my mother's house,
And I cannot go to him!
Brother, I am promised to you by the Gold of Women!
Come to me that I may see your beauty.

The 'Gold of Women' referred to here is Hathor, goddess of beauty and fertility. She was the deity who presided over Egyptian lovers, as well as over music, drunkenness and dancing. Hathor was no prude, it seems: in fact, there was definitely something of the bawd about the goddess. And it is clear that under her benign eye loving couples often slept together without going to the trouble of getting married at all.

ALL IN THE FAMILY A tomb painting from Thebes shows the family of an important functionary: Chief Workman Anherkau, the official in charge of the royal tombs during the reigns of Ramses III to Ramses VI

CONTRACEPTIVES FOR WOMEN

Egyptian doctors prescribed a variety of aids to birth control for women. Crocodile dung and honey were both recommended, and may possibly have helped to prevent sperm from passing to the womb. Another formula used powdered acacia tips. These contain gum arabic (a substance exuded by certain acacia trees) which does indeed have some contraceptive properties due to its chemical effect on sperm.

The Egyptians distinguished between women who were wives, and women who were 'with' their menfolk, cohabiting more or less as live-in lovers.

in the 20th dynasty. Beside Anherkau (with a small beard) sits his wife Wab, and with them are four of their grandchildren. Facing them is a priest bearing an offering, also probably a kinsman.

Anuket-ta-nakht, the eldest granddaughter, holds a small bird in each hand.

One of two grandsons called Anherkau, after their grandfather, bears the extra name Patjair.

Another granddaughter is named Baket-Ptah, meaning 'the servant of Ptah', the creator-god.

Henut-waty, youngest of the granddaughters shown, receives a small bird from her sister.

WOMEN'S RIGHTS

Ruled by a king and an all-male bureaucracy, Egypt nonetheless granted considerable influence to women.

EGYPTIAN WOMEN were privileged compared to their counterparts in other early civilisations such as Assyria and Greece. They could own and farm land, sell produce and arrange credit. One tomb scene shows them selling bread, fish and vegetables. In a 20th-dynasty trial, when a wife is questioned about how she got the means to buy servants, she replies with confidence: 'I bought them in exchange for produce from my garden.'

In theory at least, men and women were equal in the eyes of the law. Women were responsible for their own actions, and could be taken to court to answer for them in person (unlike some other societies of the period, where a male guardian spoke for them). Among the law cases discovered at Deir el-Medina are accusations against women for non-payment, neglect, illegal sale and theft. A woman called Heria, for example, faced trial for the theft of some tools. Despite her denials, a search of her home revealed the missing implements along with some stolen temple goods. Her fate is

FIELD WORK A woman sows seed as her husband ploughs, and gathers corn behind him as he harvests the crop. Above: a princess stands between the colossal sculpted feet of Ramses II.

not known – her crime seems to have been too grave to be dealt with in a village court, and she was packed off to face sentence by a higher authority.

Not only did women have the same property rights and legal rights as men, they were entitled to a rare degree of human respect. A passage in Egypt's wisdom literature (a collection of texts on morals and behaviour) advises: 'Don't give orders to your wife in her house when you know she is doing a good job. Don't say to her, "Where is it? Get it!", when she has put it in the right place. Watch in silence. Then you will recognise her skill.'

It would be wrong, though, to imagine that the women of ancient Egypt possessed genuine and total social equality. The Egyptians held profound beliefs about the difference between male and female principles, and these ran through every aspect of life. Man was as different from woman as the god Osiris was from the goddess Isis: both sexes had their own mystique. For example, the sun was male in the Egyptian language. Since the monarch represented the sun god on earth, it followed that only men

WIVES AND SERVANTS
The carved stone slab honours the wife of a workman named Kasa. Many women did humble work.
Right: an Egyptian serving girl carries a jar.

DAILY GRIND
A tomb model depicts a woman grinding corn for bread.

could be king. As a result, even those queens who ruled Egypt had to claim to be 'king' in order to enjoy royal power. And since the sun god's authority passed down through the pharaoh to his priests and ministers, they too had to be male.

Women were excluded from the ruling bureaucracy and from the temple elite, although there is some evidence of female literacy and of women being employed as scribes. Both sexes

worked in the fields, but while the men wielded the sickles at harvest time the women only followed, picking up the fallen ears. There seems to have been a general ban on women carrying blades, which were seen as emblems of masculinity. For example, women often worked as bakers and brewers but not as butchers, whose job involved the slaughter of animals.

Perhaps the most curious prohibition applied to the laundry trade. Women were not supposed to wash the laundry – at least not on a professional basis. The ban may have stemmed from the fact that washing clothes was a job traditionally done on the riverbank where crocodiles were a serious threat. Coping with crocodiles was a man's job.

It is hard to avoid the conclusion that, well respected though they were, Egypt's women occupied a secondary position in relation to the men. In the land of the pharaohs as throughout most of human history they were perceived first and foremost as wives and mothers. And they learned their role at a young age. An Egyptian spell designed to protect a baby contains the words: 'Are you warm in the nest? Are you hot in the bush? Is your mother with you? Is there no sister to fan you?' That last question is expressive. Even in childhood, women were expected to nurture and to serve.

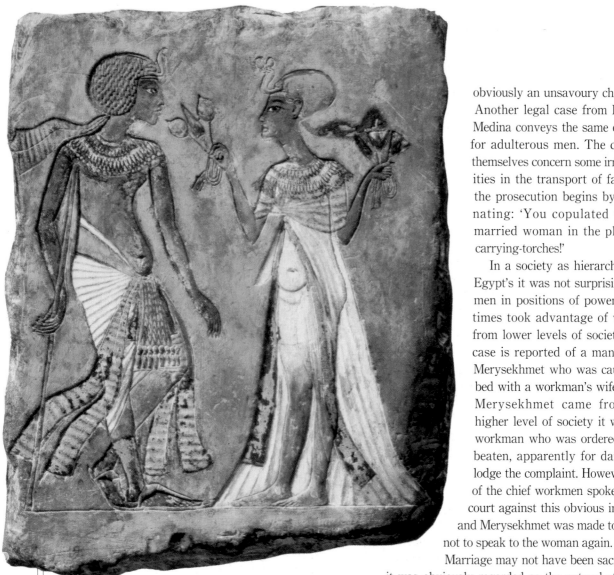

A Walk in the Garden Unlike their predecessors, the pharaoh Akhenaten and his queen, Nefertiti, were often shown in private moments of domestic life.

However, since there was no wedding ceremony in either case, the precise difference between them is hard to define. Whatever the distinction, it is obvious that sexual attitudes were fairly permissive.

'PANEB SLEPT WITH THE LADY TUY'

Making love to another man's wife, however, was frowned upon. A papyrus from the workmen's village Deir el-Medina lists the accusations made against a bullying foreman called Paneb. Charges range from bribery, threats and stealing to the following: 'Paneb slept with the Lady Tuy, when she was the wife of the workman Kenna; he slept with the Lady Hunero, when she was with Pendua; he slept with the Lady Hunero, when she was with Hesysunebef.' Paneb was obviously an unsavoury character. Another legal case from Deir el-Medina conveys the same distaste for adulterous men. The charges themselves concern some irregularities in the transport of fats, but the prosecution begins by fulminating: 'You copulated with a married woman in the place-of-carrying-torches!'

In a society as hierarchical as Egypt's it was not surprising that men in positions of power sometimes took advantage of women from lower levels of society. The case is reported of a man called Merysekhmet who was caught in bed with a workman's wife. Since Merysekhmet came from the higher level of society it was the workman who was ordered to be beaten, apparently for daring to lodge the complaint. However, one of the chief workmen spoke out in court against this obvious injustice and Merysekhmet was made to swear not to speak to the woman again.

Marriage may not have been sacred but it was obviously regarded as the natural state for men and women. A document known as the *Instructions of Ani,* a collection of do's and don'ts that was in circulation around 1500-1000 BC, warns: 'Beware of a strange woman, one not known in her town. Do not ogle her when she goes by, do not make love to her. A deep water whose course is unknown, such is a woman away from her husband.' Though the Egyptians granted more respect to the female sex than many ancient peoples, a wholly unattached woman remained an object of some suspicion. She was an outsider – a temptress.

The lone woman was also vulnerable, and Egyptian writings convey the impression that widows were a particularly disadvantaged group. When an official boasted of his good works he would describe himself as a feeder of the hungry, a clother of the naked and a helper of the widow. 'Do not be greedy for a cubit of land, nor encroach on the boundaries of a widow,' runs a piece of advice from the New

MEN'S THOUGHTS ON WOMEN

DESPITE the generally respected position that women held in Egyptian society, men were still capable of making pointed remarks about them. The *Instructions of Onkhsheshonqy* advise:

'Do not open your heart to your wife. What you have said goes into the street!'

'Let your wife see your wealth. Do not trust her with it!'

'Instructing a woman is like having a sack of sand whose side is split open!'

From the *Instructions of Onkhsheshonqy*. Preserved in a Ptolemaic papyrus, although composed earlier.

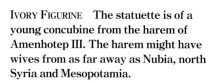

IVORY FIGURINE **The statuette is of a young concubine from the harem of Amenhotep III. The harem might have wives from as far away as Nubia, north Syria and Mesopotamia.**

Kingdom *Instructions of Amenemipet* (*c.*1250 BC). More generally, any woman seems to have been in danger if she went about without an escort. Among his achievements, Ramses III claimed that: 'I enabled the woman of Egypt to go her way, her journeys being extended where she wanted, without any other person assaulting her on the road.' It is a noble boast – but it also carries the implication that under normal circumstances Egyptian women who went out alone faced the same dangers of assault, kidnap or rape that they have faced in just about every era.

The partnership between Egyptian husbands and wives should not be overstated. Polygamy was legal, although few men seem to have taken advantage of this right. Perhaps they were discouraged by the fear of having to pay maintenance several times over. Certainly, the only known cases of polygamy come from Egypt's wealthier classes.

The pharaohs – acting for diplomatic reasons – had a number of wives, marrying daughters sent to them by foreign rulers, in order to seal their allegiance. At her height, when the country extended from the 4th Nile cataract in Sudan to Syria (*c.*1570-1070 BC), Egypt was the most powerful state in the Near Eastern world, and many a lesser monarch did not shrink from sending a daughter, along with other tributes, to the god-king. Ramses II took two Hittite princesses as brides, the first marriage taking place after the Egyptian armies had devastated the land of Hatti in Anatolia (modern Turkey and northern

Syria), where the Hittites lived: 'Now after they saw their land in this miserable state under the great power of the lord of the Two Lands, then the great prince of Hatti said to his soldiers and his courtiers: "Now see this! Our land is devastated. Let us strip ourselves of all our possessions, and with my oldest daughter in front of them, let us carry peace offerings to the Good God (the pharaoh), that he may give us peace, that we may live." Then he caused his oldest daughter to be brought, the costly tribute before her

MAN AND WIFE
Prince Rahotep and his wife Nofret depicted in painted limestone statues of the 4th dynasty. They were a couple of consequence, and the statues show considerable artistry.

**HAPPY EVENT Egyptian mothers
sometimes gave birth to their
children in a special isolation pavilion, erected
on the rooftop, in the garden or the courtyard. Right: the carving shows a woman
giving birth as she kneels on two bricks.**

consisting of gold and silver, many great ores, innumerable horses, cattle, sheep and goats.'

The grand procession was duly led into Egypt where the daughter of the Hittite king was led into the presence of the pharaoh. With suitable pomp, she was given the Egyptian name Maathorneferura, and made the king's principal wife.

This was an honour. Even in cases where Egyptian lords had several wives, one was usually named as the main wife and enjoyed special status. Lowlier members of the royal household included batches of maidens who accompanied foreign wives as maidservants. Some may also have ended up as household servants, say, or as weavers in textile workshops, while others were probably married off to government officials.

Multiple wives created all kinds of tensions within the royal household. Ramses III (1182-1151 BC) was the victim of a harem plot. The plot seems to have

An Egyptian Mother in Childbirth

THE SKY was still dark when Aneksi awoke, but a smudge of purple light on the eastern horizon signalled that dawn was at hand. It was summer, and she had been sleeping with her husband, Sety, on the flat roof of their mud-brick house. He was still dozing peacefully enough, but something now stirred in Aneksi that made even fitful slumber impossible. She felt sick, and at first thought that she must have eaten something that disagreed with her. Or perhaps it had disagreed with the baby that she carried in her heavy belly?

Aneksi rose with some difficulty from her rush mattress and rubbed at her swollen abdomen, praying as she had prayed countless times before that this child would survive. She had lost one baby – a girl, born dead – during the previous summer. Now she fervently invoked the goddesses Hathor and Taweret to protect the new life within her. She felt herself tugging at the little wooden fertility charm that hung around her neck, gripping it so tightly that it bit into her palm. And suddenly she knew. She had come to her term – the child was due.

Quickly, she wakened Sety and told him to fetch her mother and sister. Then she took up her mattress and moved it into the childbed arbour – a little pavilion which they had set up on the roof, using long papyrus stalks, rush matting, greenery and garlands of lotus. There were cushions in there, a stool cut from a palm-tree stump, and various other comforts. By the time her mother and sister arrived, the labour was well under way. 'Be brave,' they told her. 'It won't be long, Amun willing.' All through the morning, though, Aneksi experienced intense labour pangs. Her sister gave her water constantly, for it had become very hot – and brought beer, too, to help to dull the pain. Meanwhile, her mother, murmuring prayers and words of reassurance, massaged her belly with soothing oils.

At midday, just as Aneksi was beginning to feel that the ordeal was more than she could bear, she felt the overwhelming urge to push. So, with her sister supporting her from behind, she took up a squatting position over two large bricks specially placed on the floor. The gap between would give her mother a little extra space to help ease the delivery.

'It is coming', her mother called suddenly as, wailing with the effort – and with pure exultation too – Aneksi began to give birth to her child. After the long labour, these last stages came with surprising speed. 'A girl!' She heard her mother say. 'And just see what a healthy baby!' As if in answer, the newborn let out a mewling cry that seemed to Aneksi the most beautiful sound on earth. Instinctively, she brought the baby to her breast. It was some time before she spoke. Then, smiling quietly, she said, 'I shall call her Senebtese', a name that meant simply 'She is healthy'.

When the cord had been cut, they cleansed and bathed the baby, and took her to the doorway for Sety to admire. But neither Aneksi nor the child left the arbour. Both needed a period of rest and care, and the shady little pavilion was to remain their home for many days to come.

DIVINE ASSISTANCE An Egyptian mother gives birth, flanked by images of the goddess Hathor.

been instigated by a royal woman called Tiy, acting with her son, other palace women and a small group of palace officials. When he discovered the conspiracy, the pharaoh ordered Tiy's son – his own child – to commit suicide. Six women and 40 male members of

POPULAR GOD This carved image depicts Bes, a stumpy little deity invoked during childbirth. The tambourine is perhaps used to ward off evil spirits.

the pharaoh's household also paid for their crime with their lives, either through execution or compulsory suicide.

Such incidents were certainly not unique, but for obvious reasons, threats to the pharaoh's life and the internal quarrels of the royal house would have been kept as closely guarded secrets. An official of the reign of Pepy I (*c*.2332-2283 BC), some 1000 years before Ramses III, records that he was ordered by the king to oversee the trial of one of the king's wives. The crime is not specified – and all was carried out in total secrecy. Such events were probably more common than the scanty evidence suggests.

CHILDBIRTH AND PREGNANCY TESTS
The main purpose of marriage was, of course, to have children. Medical texts gave a wealth of advice on how to find out whether a woman was fertile, or pregnant, for these matters were of key importance. Some of the suggestions are basically sensible, such as taking the woman's pulse, checking the colour of the skin and eyes, and testing for morning sickness. Other predictions belonged to the realm of magic while containing some tantalising hints of a scientific foundation. For example, the following is an ancient Egyptian test for pregnancy:

LUCKY CHARM
A wooden amulet, depicting a mother and baby, was worn in the hope of a trouble-free birth. Left: a tomb painting from Thebes shows a mother carrying her baby in a linen sling.

You shall put wheat and barley into purses of cloth.
The woman shall pass her water on it, every day.
If both sprout, she will bear.
If the wheat sprouts, she will bear a boy.
If the barley sprouts, she will bear a girl.
If neither sprouts, she will not bear at all.

At first glance it seems pure hocus-pocus. Yet modern pregnancy testing is done by urine samples, to discover whether a particular hormone is present. Tests made in the 1960s by Professor Ghalioungui of Cairo's Ein Shams University suggested that the hormones in the urine of pregnant women *can* cause barley and wheat to germinate. It worked in about 40 per cent of cases, while the urine of women who were not pregnant prevented the seed from growing. Not surprisingly, however, there was found to be no relationship between male babies and sprouting wheat, or female babies and sprouting barley.

Just as expectant mothers do today, Egyptian women massaged their abdomen with oil during pregnancy. They did this partly to ease the forthcoming birth and partly to prevent stretch marks. Wealthy women used oil obtained from the horseradish tree *(Moringa aptera),* which they stored in special vases made of calcite – Egyptian alabaster. These were shaped to resemble pregnant women, standing or squatting naked, with the hands placed on the abdomen as though rubbing it.

Mothers gave birth standing or squatting, sometimes on a pair of large bricks to assist the helpers in delivery. One reference to them comes in an ancient Egyptian story of a man punished by the goddess Meresger: 'I squatted on bricks like the woman in labour', he says. The delivery might take place in a special pavilion, and the mother was usually attended by two women, one kneeling in front and one holding her from behind. Professional midwives were known, but the vocation was thought to be unclean and was not highly esteemed. It is likely that in most families, the older female relatives normally performed the service.

FAMILY GROUP **The wife of a dwarf named Seneb puts her arms around his shoulders. Their two children stand in front.**

In a society without modern medicine childbirth was fraught with dangers and the spectre of death lingered over mother and baby alike. A dead child in one inscription proclaims: 'Harm is what befell me when I was but a child! I was driven from childhood too early! Turned away from my house as a youngster, before I had my fill in it! The dark, a child's terror, engulfed me, while the breast was in my mouth!' Nobody in ancient Egypt was guaranteed a ripe old age, as another inscription made clear:

Do not say: 'I am too young to be taken away'
for you do not know your death.
When death comes he steals the infant
from the arms of his mother,
just like him who has reached old age.

THE ROLE OF CHILDREN

A child's life was fraught with dangers ranging from snakebite to stomach infection.

Egyptian parents hung charms around their youngsters to protect them from misfortune,

and had spells cast to ward off disease.

WHILE EXCAVATING the pyramid builders' town of Kahun in the Faiyum, the British archaeologist Flinders Petrie came upon the bodies of many newborn infants buried, sometimes two or three to a box, under the house floors. His assumption was that they were unwanted babies, and he wrote in his journal for April 1889: 'Unlucky babes seem to have been conveniently put out of the way by stuffing them into a toilet case or clothes box and digging a hole in the floor for them . . . I fear these discoveries do not reflect much credit on the manners and customs of the small officials of the 12th dynasty.'

Certainly, unwanted pregnancies were known in ancient Egypt: medical texts gave advice on contraception and how to bring on an abortion. But it is more likely that Petrie's hapless babes were victims of Egypt's high infant mortality rate. A multitude of ail-

MEDICINE BOTTLE
Flasks shaped like a nursing mother may have been used to hold mothers' milk for sick children.

PREHISTORIC FIGURE
This prehistoric figure, carved from ebony, dates back to the 4th millennium BC. Like many Egyptian mothers, the woman is carrying her child on her left hip.

ments threatened mother and child, in particular childbirth and intestinal infections. It was small wonder that women prayed to the gods for a safe delivery, seeking help especially from Taweret, the pregnant hippopotamus goddess, known as 'she who brings down the birth waters'. And there were spells which were supposed to work by identifying the child with the god Horus, son of Isis:

Come down, placenta, come down, come down!
I am Horus who conjures in order that she who is
giving birth becomes better than she was,
as if she was already delivered . . .
Look, Hathor will lay her hand on her
with an amulet of health!
I am Horus who saves her.

TRIPLET PHARAOHS

Practical measures were also taken. Among the folk stories in an ancient Egyptian book known as *Tales of Wonder* is that of Ruddedit, a woman who gives birth to triplets who all become pharaohs. After the birth of each baby, for example, when the umbilical cord has been cut, the newborn infant is washed and laid on a pillow of cloth. Then Ruddedit, the mother, undergoes a 'cleansing of 14 days'. This presumably means an

SPELL TO WARD OFF INFECTION

*Come on out, visitor from the darkness, who crawls along with
your nose and face on the back of your head, not knowing why
you are here!*
Have you come to kiss this child? I forbid you to do so!
Have you come to cosset this child? I forbid you to!
Have you come to do it harm? I forbid this!

*Have you come to take it away from me? I forbid you to!
I have made ready for its protection a potion from the
poisonous* afat *herb, from garlic which is bad for you,
from honey which is sweet for the living but bitter for the dead,
from the droppings and entrails of fish and beast
and from the spine of the perch.*

From the papyrus *The Spells for Mother and Child,* **which gave advice on childcare.**

isolation period, when rest and care were provided to prevent postnatal infections.

Because marriage was such an informal affair the Egyptians had no concept of illegitimacy. The natural father and mother were always considered to be a child's parents. Babies were named at birth, rather than in some later ceremony, and it was generally the

mother who made the choice. If the newborn reminded her of her husband she might make reference to the fact with a name such as Etfanch ('His father lives'). Or she might state the father's nationality or profession: Pakharu was 'the Syrian' while Pakapu was 'the Birdcatcher'. Many names honoured a god: Rahotep meant 'Re [the sun god] is content', Amenhotep was

ROYAL PRINCESSES Almond-eyed and shaven-headed, two daughters of the pharaoh Akhenaten take their ease on
richly patterned cushions. The painting is an unusually intimate depiction of a domestic scene.

WILLS AND INHERITANCE

WHEN Egyptian parents died, their children seem to have shared the inheritance equally, irrespective of their gender. Disputes over the division of property were rare but they did occur, so it was sometimes necessary for a will to be made. This might happen if, say, a father or mother wanted to disinherit children whom they regarded as less than dutiful. Additionally, there was a very important tradition associated with inheritance. Sons and daughters who wanted to claim their share had to help with the burial rites. The Egyptians made elaborate provision for the afterlife and the funeral arrangements must have been both costly and time-consuming.

One legal document describes the case of a woman called Tagemy. On her death, she was buried by her loyal son Huy, with no assistance from any of the other children. As a result, Huy inherited all his mother's belongings. When he died, however, his brothers and sisters laid claim to a portion of his estate, insisting that Huy had not made the funeral arrangements alone. Huy's son, who risked losing some of his inheritance, was having none of this. As he noted: 'Let the possessions be given to him who buries.' Other precedents survive from ancient Egypt, demonstrating a clear connection between performing the burial and being the heir. This must help to explain the lavish tomb-building and tomb-furnishing habits of the upper classes. Sons and daughters who failed to play their part in the burial risked losing every penny of their inheritance.

ALL IN THE FAMILY The 20th-dynasty pharaoh, Ramses III (shown here with one of his children) named his sons after the sons of Ramses II.

'Amun [the sky god] is content' and Tuthmose was 'Thoth [the god of wisdom] lives'. If a child was born on one of the days of the great festivals, he or she might be given a name alluding to the fact. For example, Mutemwia meant 'Mut is in the barque', referring to the day when the statue of the god Mut was carried in its barque along the Nile.

Other names celebrated the happy occasion of the birth, such as Haunefer ('Beautiful Day') and Duatnefret ('Beautiful Morning'). A touching affection is displayed by some of the names chosen: Miu was 'Tomcat', Mytsereu was 'Kitten', and the Egyptian fondness for animals is reflected in other names such as 'Frog', 'Mouse' and 'Gazelle'. Another trait was the Egyptians' habit of shortening names, so that Amenemopet became Ipy, for example, and Amenhotep, Huy.

Names went in fashions and many babies were simply given that of the ruling pharaoh, which must have caused confusion in everyday life. Under the 12th Dynasty it became fashionable for the officials in the household of any great man to call themselves and their children after their master. The German pioneer of Egyptology, Adolf Erman, discovered that in one Middle Kingdom province two-thirds of all the officials bore the same name as the governing prince.

Children, of course, were objects of love in the family, but they were also an important asset.

FOREIGN WIVES A Nubian woman captive with her children. Egyptian men sometimes took Nubian wives, which may explain why boys and girls received names such as Panehesy and Tanehesy, meaning 'the Nubian'.

enough to make provision for an afterlife it was the children who saw that their parents got a proper burial, making offerings at their tombs and ensuring that the appropriate rituals were carried out for their spirits. 'It is proper to create people. Happy the man whose people are many, he is saluted on account of his offspring', runs one ancient text, while another declares: 'Love your wife with ardour. Gladden her heart as long as you live. She is a fertile field for her lord.'

Childless couples prayed with fervour for offspring, often seeking help from their own dead relatives. Believing that the departed were still in some sort of contact with this world, the Egyptians petitioned them with

Not only were they supposed to work for their parents or bring home wages, they also provided security in the parents' old age. Even after a person's death they had a role to play, for in the households wealthy

such requests as: 'Cause that there be born to me a healthy male child.' Spells were inscribed on the underside of scarabs (the sacred dung beetle that was the symbol of the sun god), and if all else failed, the childless still had the option of adopting, as a letter written by a very petulant 20th-dynasty scribe makes clear: 'What's the meaning of your getting into such a bad mood as this, that nobody's words can enter your ears because of your inflated self-esteem? You are not a man since you are unable to make your wives pregnant like your fellow men. A further matter: You are exceedingly stingy. You give no one anything. As for him who has no children, he adopts an orphan . . .' The passage continues with the observation that the orphan will then be the one to 'pour water on one's hands, as a genuine eldest son'. Evidently, pouring water on the father's hands, probably before meals, was among the tasks expected of a dutiful son.

After the birth and the naming, a child was breast-

DOG AND MONKEY

Tomb robbers in ancient Egypt showed no respect for mummies as they searched burial places for gold. Often they would tear off a head or a limb as they ripped open the wrappings of pharaohs and their queens. They even played macabre jokes. One group of thieves unwrapped carefully mummified bodies of a monkey and a dog and propped them up to look as if they were chatting to one another. Three thousand years later when archaeologists opened the burial shaft, the creatures were still in conversation.

HOLY MOTHER The goddess Isis nurses the infant Horus. Since the pharaoh was considered an incarnation of Horus, the statue has a particular significance, confirming the king's divine status.

fed by the mother up to the age of three. It is a long time by modern Western standards, but it is not particularly unusual in other societies. One advantage is that a woman reduces her chances of becoming pregnant again while she is lactating – breastfeeding is a primitive form of birth control. Toddlers as well as babies are shown being breastfed in Egyptian scenes, and it is clear that suckling was done in public without any embarrassment. Should the supply of milk be inadequate to the child's needs, Egyptian doctors recommended massaging the mother's back with oil in which the dorsal fin of a Nile perch had been stewed. If the child was sick, the mother was supposed to eat a mouse: the creature's bones

were then placed in a little canvas bag tied with seven knots and hung as a talisman around the infant's neck.

Most women suckled their own offspring, but wet nurses were employed in the wealthier households, and the legal relations between them and the parents were sometimes formalised in written contracts. Within the pharaoh's palace, the wet nurse acquired a powerful position because of her intimacy with the royal children. Suckling was, in fact, an activity charged with religious significance. Statuettes showing the goddess Isis suckling her son Horus must have had the same potent appeal to worshippers, embodying the ideal of divine motherhood. In art, pharaohs were sometimes shown sucking at the breast of one or another goddess, as if they were drinking in divinity along with the goddess's milk.

Children were certainly drinking in a degree of safety from infection while they were being suckled. Czech researchers investigating infant mortality in one Egyptian cemetery discovered a higher death rate among three- to four-year-old children than among the younger age group who would still have been fed at the breast. The switch to solid foods was accompanied by a greater risk of intestinal infections.

THE LOCK OF YOUTH

Mothers carried their babies and toddlers in a linen sling that left their own arms free to get on with work around the house or in the fields. Amulets were hung around their youngsters' necks to guard them against the evil eye, and mothers also sought magical protection by wearing little cylindrical pendants made of wood or metal. Inside were tiny papyrus rolls, tightly folded and bound with flax, bearing spells written in hieratic script (a quick way of writing hieroglyphs). These might be directed against anything from snakebite, leprosy or blindness to false accusation or even the common cold. There were spells against spirits and sorcery, too – especially the sorcery of foreigners. All speaks of an intense concern for the well-being of young children, and a sense that the world around them bristled with menace.

Children often wore nothing but their pendant or

EYEWITNESS

A BOY'S BEST FRIEND

THE SCRIBE ANI advises adult children to show a proper respect for their mothers in his collections of *Instructions*:

Double the food your mother gave you,
Support her as she supported you;
She had a heavy load in you,
But she did not abandon you.
When you were born after your months,
She was yoked to you,
Her breast in your mouth for three years.
As you grew and your excrement disgusted,
She was not disgusted, saying 'What shall I do?'
When she sent you to school
And you were taught to write,
She kept watch over you daily,
With bread and beer in her house.

From a papyrus dating from the 18th-21st dynasties.

FAMILY OUTING An 18th-dynasty tomb painting shows the nobleman Nebamun hunting in the marshes with his wife, daughter – and pet cat. Right: a girl carrying a bird, either as a pet or a religious offering. Notice her 'lock of youth'.

amulet, for in the long hot Egyptian summer nakedness was regarded as perfectly natural in youngsters. Among girls, nudity was common until they reached puberty. Among boys, nakedness was even more widespread – many youths would grow up to work in no more than a loincloth even as adults. Nonetheless, some carefully made children's clothes have survived. When King Tutankhamun's tomb was opened up, the discoverers found nearly 50 garments belonging to the boy pharaoh, as well as a multitude of gloves,

scarfs, belts and headgear. Among the clothes was an exquisite baby's robe made of finely spun and bleached linen. It took the form of an adult-length tunic having a neck opening large enough only for the head of a new-born baby. Measuring over 5 ft (1.5 m) long, the garment is reckoned to have taken 3000 hours to make. If, as seems likely, it was worn by Tutankhamun soon after his birth, it must have involved the maker working 11 hours a day over a period of nine months.

The articles in his wardrobe cannot, of course, be regarded as typical everyday wear. But other children's clothes have also been recovered from ancient Egypt. One of these is a child's pleated linen dress (now in the Petrie Museum, University College, London), which is reckoned to be the oldest garment in the world. Dating back to the reign of King Djet in the 1st dynasty, about 2800 BC, it probably belonged to a child of about ten,

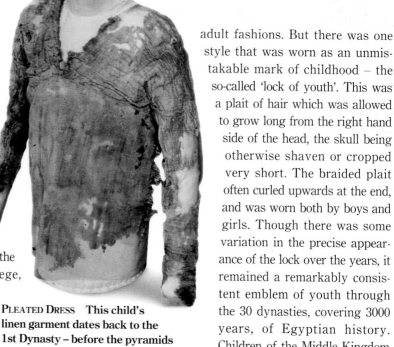

PLEATED DRESS   This child's linen garment dates back to the 1st Dynasty – before the pyramids were built. It is reckoned to be the oldest surviving garment in the world.

and had obviously been worn because it was creased around the armpits and elbows. It was, moreover, inside out, having caught around the narrow wrists as it was pulled off over the head.

Children's detachable linen sleeves have also been found. Sleeves appear as individual items in Egyptian laundry lists, and must have been particularly useful for youngsters' clothes which do get worn around the elbows (as the 1st-dynasty dress testifies). Presumably the sleeves were kept off for normal wear, and attached only when the weather turned cold – and winters can be bitterly so in Egypt.

Children who go about clothed in Egyptian paintings often wear miniature versions of the prevailing adult fashions. But there was one style that was worn as an unmistakable mark of childhood – the so-called 'lock of youth'. This was a plait of hair which was allowed to grow long from the right hand side of the head, the skull being otherwise shaven or cropped very short. The braided plait often curled upwards at the end, and was worn both by boys and girls. Though there was some variation in the precise appearance of the lock over the years, it remained a remarkably consistent emblem of youth through the 30 dynasties, covering 3000 years, of Egyptian history. Children of the Middle Kingdom used to hang a fish-shaped amulet from the end of the plait as a charm against drowning, and a number of these have survived. They depict the catfish, *Synodontis batensoda,* and are wrought from gold or silver and inlaid with turquoise, carnelian or lapis lazuli.

Artists used the lock of youth to indicate that a figure in one of their paintings was supposed to be a youngster. And there was another convention too: children were often shown with the right index finger stuck in the corner of the mouth, where it served as a dummy. Young Egyptians, it seems, were congenital thumb-suckers (or finger-suckers): here, perhaps, was a further effect of prolonged breastfeeding.

WHIP TOPS, SKITTLES AND PUPPETS

For amusement, children had whip tops, made from circular pieces of wood flattened at one end and tapering to a point at the other. They also played with tip-cats, sticks of wood pointed at each end, which were hit into the air with a bat or another stick, and batted again before they reached the ground to see how far they would

PLAYTHINGS   Egyptian children had a wealth of amusements. The draughtboard was made during the New Kingdom era. The wheeled horse is later, dating to the Roman period.

HUMAN WHIRLIGIG Two youths standing in the middle spin their companions around them in the 'star game'.

travel. The winner was the child whose tip-cat went farthest (a very similar game, known as 'Peggy', is still played in the north of England today). There were ball games too. Some balls were crudely shaped from wood, others more carefully fashioned from panels of leather, linen or reed which were sewn together and stuffed. From the Middle Kingdom town of Kahun, archaeologists have recovered one leather ball, stuffed with dried grass, which had obviously cracked at some time and been carefully re-stitched – a tribute to the extent to which its ancient owner must have valued it.

The Egyptians played a version of skittles. From a child's grave at Naqada archaeologists recovered a complete set consisting of nine skittles, with four balls of porphyry which had to be rolled through a marble gate. The Egyptians also made ingenious human and animal figures with moving parts. One of these, for example, is a wooden figure shown grinding corn – a tug on the cord makes the outstretched arms go up and down. A wooden crocodile with a snapping lower jaw is another example, and a third is a cat-like creature with crystal eyes and a movable jaw fitted with teeth of bronze. The most impressive of these playthings, though, is a group of four small ivory figures representing naked, dancing pygmies with highly expressive

faces. One stands on his own, with his hands together in a clapping gesture. The other three are grouped together on a single base. Tugging at cords caused them to dance in a jerky fashion, even executing full pirouettes. This was clearly a treasured possession, and it had at some time been painstakingly repaired with tiny dowels.

Egyptian girls amused themselves with painted wooden dolls that had movable limbs. They had rag dolls, too, with wigs of mud beads and wardrobes of clothes that included complete changes of outfit. In one house at Kahun, archaeologists found a large quantity of doll's hair cut in 6 in (15 cm) lengths of fine flax thread which was rolled with mud so that it could be fitted onto the doll's head. The house where the find was made became known as the 'toymaker's shop', and may well have been a centre for a local doll-making industry.

The most sophisticated toys were, of course, only for the enjoyment of the privileged children of the leisured classes. But a wealth of simple clay figurines have also been found, including little models of

LEAPFROG Dating from the 5th or 6th dynasty, this painted limestone statuette was found in a tomb at Giza and may represent leapfrog.

39

hippopotamuses, crocodiles, apes and pigs all fashioned from grey Nile mud. Many are so crudely formed that they must have probably been shaped by the children themselves.

A HUMAN ROUNDABOUT

Girls and boys rarely play together in Egyptian paintings or sculpture, but there are some exceptions. One of these is a painted limestone statuette showing a naked boy astride a kneeling girl who is clothed. It looks very much like a representation of leapfrog. Certainly, the young enjoyed vigorous games of this sort. One favourite is still played in Egypt and the Near East and known as *khazza lawizza* – 'jumping over the goose' in modern Arabic. Two children sit face to face with arms and legs outstretched to form a human hurdle over which a third child has to leap. Naked boys play the game in Egyptian tomb scenes. One activity has earned itself the nickname of the 'star game' from scholars, and involves a kind of living merry-go-round. Two boys stand in the middle with arms outstretched, holding others who lean back on their heels and are whirled around them. In ancient

Egypt, the game was called 'erecting the wine arbour'. Girls seem occasionally to have played it with boys, but they are more often shown in the company of their own sex, sometimes dancing, sometimes performing back-flips or somersaults. Whether the girls depicted are young professional dancers is not entirely clear. What is obvious, though, is that the rigid, walking figures seen in so many Egyptian paintings convey a false solemnity. The Egyptians liked to see young people leap and dance.

Some Egyptian scenes are almost like frames from a strip cartoon, with bubble captions to explain what is going on. One of them shows a tug of war between two lines of three boys each. The captains stand heel to heel, gripping each other at the wrist and straining backwards with their upper bodies. Behind them their companions form a human chain, each holding on to the one in front with both hands around the waist. At a given command they start to pull, and their shouts are recorded in hieroglyphic captions above the teams. 'Your arm is much stronger than his. Don't give in to him', comes the cry from one side. In response, an opponent bawls out: 'My side is stronger than yours. Hold them firmly, my friend.'

Dogs were kept for hunting from about 4000 BC onwards, and they also appear as household pets in tomb finds. The Egyptians gave their dogs names:

'MIAOU'

The immortal 'miaou' – or something very like it – seems to have been the cry of all cats since the dawn of recorded time. The Egyptian word for cat was *miu* or *mii* (feminine *miit*), meaning he or she who mews.

'Ebony', 'Black', 'Big', and in some cases more grandiose titles such as 'Steering-Oar of the Lion' (a reference to this particular pet's tail). The greyhound was among the favourite breeds. A 5th-dynasty official called Ptahhotep insisted on keeping his three greyhounds at his side while his musicians played for him – despite the fact that they howled throughout the performance.

The Egyptian love of animals is obvious from their paintings, and the cat, in particular, was revered as a divine creature associated with the sun. The goddess Bastet was worshipped in her guise as a cat, and her immense festival at Bubastis was among the most frenzied events in the Egyptian calendar. Cats were domesticated considerably later than dogs – around 2000 BC – and they start to crop up regularly in New Kingdom tomb paintings of family life about 500 years later. The Egyptian cat was in fact the ancestor of the common house cat of

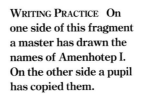

WRITING PRACTICE On one side of this fragment a master has drawn the names of Amenhotep I. On the other side a pupil has copied them.

western Europe, reaching ancient Greece and Rome and spreading north from there, probably interbreeding to some extent with Europe's indigenous wild cat.

Cats are sometimes portrayed in Egyptian paintings playing with pet monkeys, another household favourite. The Egyptians originally imported baboons and monkeys from the south, but later they bred them in captivity at home. In paintings, a monkey can occasionally be glimpsed under a chair, pulling an onion to bits, or tipping out the contents of a basket. A number of lords had pet monkeys represented with them in their tombs, and a courtier named Nebemchut is known to have owned two shaggy baboons which he used to take with him when he inspected his workforce.

CHILDREN OF THE NILE Like all youngsters, Egyptian boys and girls devised their own pastimes, romped, danced and played with their toys. But childhood was also the time in which they were introduced to the rigours of working life. Right: a brickmaker teaches his son the basics of his craft. To make mud bricks – the building blocks of ancient Egypt – a mixture of mud and chopped straw was tipped into a wooden mould. When the mixture had been pressed down firmly, the mould was lifted from the moist brick and another was laid by its side.

THE CAT: A DIVINE PET

Beautiful and aloof, cats were highly esteemed in ancient Egypt.

Most modern domestic breeds descend from Egyptian ancestors.

HERODOTUS, the Greek historian, reported that when an Egyptian house was on fire, the family were more concerned about the fate of their cats than their other possessions. He was writing in the 5th century BC, by which time the cat had become not only loved as a household pet but revered, too, as a living link with the gods.

Two species of cat are native to the country, the tan-coloured swamp or jungle cat, *Felis chaus*, and its smaller relation the African wild cat, *Felis silvestris libyca*. Examination of cat mummies has revealed that the vast majority were *Felis silvestris libyca*, and this is assumed to have been the domestic cat chiefly known in ancient Egypt.

It is likely that cats from the wilds were first welcomed by the Egyptians to destroy the rats and mice that infested the granaries on country estates and the communal silos in towns. The domestication process may have begun as early as 4000 BC, and it is not hard to imagine that the first wild cats, slinking into settlements by night, came to recognise the grain stores as profitable hunting grounds. Discovering the raiders' value in killing vermin, the Egyptians may have left out scraps of food to encourage them to return. And so, perhaps, the ancient bonding of cats and humans began.

From about 2000 BC Egyptian scribes started using the image of the cat,

BRONZE STATUETTE
Large numbers of bronze figures of cats were produced after about 1000 BC. They reflect the huge popularity of the cult of the cat goddess, Bastet.

squatting alert on its haunches, as a sign in their hieroglyphic alphabet, in which symbols and pictures represented objects and events. And over the next few hundred years, cats started to make themselves at home in Egyptian houses. A domestic species gradually came into being, content to give up a measure of independence for the food and shelter on offer among humans.

Cats crop up regularly in New Kingdom tomb paintings of family life. They almost always appear sitting under the chair of the wife, as if to signify a special relationship with the mistress of the house. Cats also turned out to have some surprise uses: they appear in scenes of hunting in the marshes where they are shown helping the hunters by flushing fowl out of thickets of reed and papyrus. They may have been employed to kill snakes as well as rats and mice, the image of the sun god as a cat severing the head of a snake occurs in funerary documents. And physicians ascribed medical properties to cats. To prevent the hair from going grey, for example, doctors recommended a lotion based on the placenta of a cat.

Familiar as they became in Egyptian homes, cats never lost a hint of mystery stemming from their closeness to wild nature. And that mystery found its ultimate expression in religion. The people took to wearing amulets showing cats as protection against everyday hazards; at the same time, cats and cat-headed beings started to appear in coffin decorations. The cat was said to accompany and serve the sun god on its descent into the underworld realms of darkness and death, and became especially associated with the sun god's daughters.

The final triumph of the cat came when the city of Bubastis rose to eminence during the 22nd dynasty (945-700 BC). The city's main deity was the goddess Bastet, shown as a lioness-headed – or cat-headed – woman. Wherever she was worshipped, people also took to burying mummified cats as acts of piety. This was a time when the state and temple authorities encouraged patronage of popular deities and local animal cults as a revitalising force. In the case of Bastet, the cult meant there was a goddess in every household.

According to Herodotus, when a cat died the members of an Egyptian family shaved their eyebrows as a sign of mourning and took the dead creature to Bubastis to be embalmed and buried. An extensive cat cemetery on the site was pillaged in the 19th century, and archaeologists found only 'heaps of white bones of cats' littering the ground, along with a few bronze statuettes and cat masks. But cat cemeteries have also been identified at Saqqara, Istabl Antar, and several other places, while individual cat burials have been reported from all over Egypt. The total number of animals involved has been estimated at hundreds of thousands – possibly millions. In view of the Egyptians' regard for cats, it is disquieting to learn that a high proportion of the cat mummies

ON THE PROWL A cat steals birds' eggs in a painting from 1390 BC. Left: a mummified cat from between 664 and 332 BC.

examined were of creatures who died when only a few months old. It seems that they had been strangled or had their necks broken. No doubt the process of mummification and burial demonstrated an Egyptian's piety – but it may also have doubled as a covert way of culling unwanted kittens without incurring the wrath of the gods. Killing a cat

in normal circumstances, however, was regarded as a serious offence. Herodotus claimed that anyone who deliberately killed a sacred animal was put to death. Diodorus confirms reports of an incident which he witnessed around 59 BC. It seems that a visiting member of a Roman delegation accidentally killed a cat – and not even royal intervention could save him from being lynched by an enraged crowd.

SQUABBLING GIRLS In a detail from a busy 18th-dynasty harvest scene, two young girls fight over some of the wheat left behind by the reapers.

Children were particularly fond of birds as pets. Youngsters in Egyptian scenes often clutch a duck, a pigeon, a lapwing or some other bird in one hand. Boys had a liking for the hoopoe, a colourful bird with a gaudy feathered crest. The hoopoe is normally wild but does become tame in captivity. In contrast, the Nile geese which are carried in some paintings could have been religious offerings, for they are known to be aggressive. Nonetheless geese were certainly kept as pets – like pet monkeys, they are sometimes depicted scrapping with cats in Egyptian homes.

'HOLD HIM FIRMLY. DON'T LET HIM SWOON'

A child's life did not consist only of leapfrog, spinning tops and playing with family pets, of course. At some time between the ages of five and ten, all those boys destined for any profession that required literacy would be packed off to school. Boys were also taken into the army at an early age, and for the vast mass of the peasants and craftsmen, childhood was a period which introduced them to the daily grind of toil in the fields, the vineyards or the workshop.

From an early age, country boys and girls, for instance, helped with the gleaning. This was a job which involved no great experience – just a lot of nimble ducking to pick up ears of corn left on the ground after harvesting. Children were sent out bird-chasing too. Boys assisted the herdsmen by watching flocks and tending cattle, while girls helped around the house and looked after any younger brothers and sisters. From about the age of seven, daughters would be expected to gather fuel for the oven and to help in baking bread.

In all times and in all societies, children have been used for running errands. A riverboat kitchen hut is depicted in one Middle Kingdom tomb scene: one squatting figure is operating the roasting spit while another, holding a piece of meat, gives an order to the kitchen boy: 'Off you go and call the lads to eat,' the boy replies, 'I'll do it.' In bakeries with large ovens, it seems, boys had the job of holding the baker's feet. This was a vital precaution: one inscription describes how the baker has to lean into the hot oven while his son holds onto his feet, and 'if he slips from his son's hand, he falls to the bottom of the oven'.

For boys, the transition to adulthood was formally marked by circumcision. The operation was sometimes performed on the whole age-group of a town or village, for in one inscription a man recalls the time when 'I was circumcised together with 120 men'. It is also interesting that the Egyptian hieroglyph for a phallus shows a circumcised example.

Circumcision is clearly depicted in two scenes from a 6th-Dynasty tomb at the burial area at Saqqara. In the first picture, an assistant applies a painkilling oil or ointment to the boy's penis, while the caption reads: 'I will make it comfortable.' The second scene shows the operation itself, performed by a man known as the *ka*-priest. This was a title borne not only by priests, but also applied to various members of the household staff of a high official. The surgeon could even have been a butcher or a barber, so circumcision was not necessarily a religious ritual. Nor did it involve the removal of the whole foreskin, for Old Kingdom statues indicate that it was instead marked with a V-shaped incision. Nonetheless, the operation will have been memorable enough for any youth who endured it. The boy in the tomb scene looks distinctly queasy as the priest calls out to an assistant (who is holding the lad from behind): 'Hold him firmly. Don't let him swoon.'

YOUNG EGYPTIAN A carved wooden statue depicts the circumcision that marked the change to adulthood.

LIFE IN THE EGYPTIAN HOME

Banqueting scenes from noblemen's tombs show Egyptian home life at its most convivial. Yet, crowded with relatives, servants, pets and even livestock, an Egyptian home can have offered little expectation of privacy. Rooms were fuggy with cooking fumes and lamp smoke, with pervasive odours of baking bread and brewing beer. Small wonder that families escaped whenever possible to the fresh air of the courtyard, garden or rooftop.

THE ANATOMY OF THE HOME

The fierce desert sun determined much about the appearance of Egyptian houses.

Outside walls were whitewashed to reflect the glare, and small windows were set high up

to keep the interior as shady as possible.

HOME FOR MOST Egyptians was a box-like affair, so plain and functional that it might almost have been the work of a modern architect. Whitewashed inside and out, houses were one or two storeys high and families spent a lot of time up on the flat roof, which was reached by outside stairs. To escape the stuffy atmosphere downstairs, people cooked on the roof using portable braziers; relaxed up there under shady awnings of matted rushes; and in summer even slept on the roof to take advantage of the cool night air. The Egyptians valued the northerly breeze which they associated with the breath of Amun, the sky god. Up on the roof, a funnel-shaped vent was often installed to trap it and conduct its airstream down into the heart of the building.

The sun-dried mud bricks for house-building came in standard sizes. Strips of linen were mixed in to reinforce the longer blocks needed for lintels (rather as prestressed concrete today contains steel wires). Egypt was short of good timber for construction work, for big trees did not flourish in the arid climate. None the less, split or whole date-palm stems served well enough for the roofing beams. For flooring the builders might put down a layer of brick tiles, or content themselves with stamped earth. The closeness of the flood river meant that it could become damp underfoot and the brick walls were prone to rot at ground level. One solution was to give the walls a footing of quarried stone; another was to erect the building on the heaped-up debris of earlier mud-brick dwellings. This habit of

HOUSE AND GARDEN The whitewashed, tree-fringed dwelling belonged to an 18th-dynasty official. It was built on a raised level as a precaution against flooding. Left: a limestone model of a house dates from the New Kingdom.

building and rebuilding on the same site gave Egypt her abundant *tells* – artificial hillocks formed by the accumulated remains of successive settlements.

Once the brickwork had been completed, the builders would slap on a layer of mud plaster. The plasterers'

HOUSEHOLD PROTECTORS

GROTESQUE IMAGES of the god Bes often adorned Egyptian houses and household objects. A dwarfish, bandy-legged figure, he was considered the protector of homes and of pregnant women. Bes wore a lion's skin and was sometimes depicted carrying a sword and shield to protect the dwelling from evil. He was also shown guzzling food, or capering to music. Unlike other figures in Egyptian art, Bes appears face frontal – figures are usually seen in profile.

The other immensely popular household deity was Taweret – a pregnant hippopotamus goddess chiefly associated with childbirth and fertility. Childbirth sometimes took place in a special confinement pavilion situated in the garden or on the roof. At the settlement of Deir el-Medina, babies were born on a special brick-built platform which was situated in the household chapel, with an image of Bes presiding on the wall.

TAWERET
The pregnant hippopotamus goddess ensured fertility and protected mothers in childbirth.

floats looked much like their modern counterparts, and came in different types for rough and smooth facing. Some tools found at a pyramid workmen's town at Kahun still had the remnants of plaster on them – evidence that the ancient labourers, 4000 years ago, had omitted to clean them.

EGYPTIAN INTERIORS

The homes of the rich and the poor shared the same three basic elements: an entrance area; a central living space; and a kitchen or storerooms leading off. The central living space was the heart of the house with a fairly lofty ceiling supported on wooden pillars.

It was dark, though, for the windows were small and set high in the walls to prevent too much of the harsh desert sun from entering. The Egyptians did not use glass panes – although they made opaque glass they could not make large sheets of it; instead, to keep out dust and sand they simply covered the window openings with pieces of linen cloth. None the less, it seems to have been very fuggy in the downstairs rooms. Lamp smoke and cooking fumes spread around the house, blackening the ceilings to such an extent that they were not thought worth whitewashing. And inhaling the air caused anthracosis, a condition which results from sooty deposits in the lungs, and which has often been detected in mummies. There were other health hazards too. The small entrance area in a poor man's terraced home might well be shared with a donkey or goat and lead through to chambers crowded with children and aged relatives. Evidence suggests that in some workmen's cottages, over two dozen people were sometimes packed together. The

BUILDING WORKERS
Bricklayers used a standard brick for house-building, roughly 12 x 6 x 3 in (30 x 15 x 8 cm). There was a larger one for temples and palaces.

Egyptians were, on the whole, a fastidious people, but running a hygienic household and controlling the spread of disease cannot have been easy under these conditions. Nits have been discovered in the hair of many mummies. And ratholes have been found in the corners of rooms – stuffed up with rags and stones by the inhabitants.

Flies came in through the unglazed windows, as did mosquitoes – a particular plague in the marshy delta as the floods receded in autumn. The link between mosquitoes and malaria was not yet known, but the Egyptians were familiar enough with the misery of being bitten. According to the Greek historian Herodotus, the marsh people rigged up mosquito nets, which they improvised from their fishing nets.

Insects must have plagued rich and poor alike. But in contrast to the cramped homes of many ordinary people, the dwellings of the upper classes were spacious affairs which stood in leafy, walled gardens. They were also splendidly and imaginatively decorated. Their interior walls were often colour-washed or painted with lively scenes – sometimes of heart-stopping beauty. The 'Green Room', in the North Palace at Amarna, for example, wonderfully

ABOUT THE HOUSE The stool was probably the most common article of furniture in Egyptian homes. Three-legged tables, with wooden lampstands shaped like papyrus columns, sometimes stood in the corners of rooms.

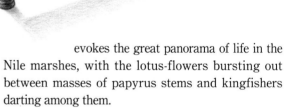

evokes the great panorama of life in the Nile marshes, with the lotus-flowers bursting out between masses of papyrus stems and kingfishers darting among them.

Wealthy citizens enjoyed the comfort of a bathroom too, although there was no running water: the bather stood on a stone slab and had water poured over him or her by a servant. A pipe then carried the waste water out through a hole in the bathroom wall

LUXURY ITEMS
Furniture for the rich was often of high quality. This chair is of wood, overlaid with gold. Other pieces were veneered, inlaid or painted in rich colours, like this chest.

A PASSION FOR GARDENING

THE EGYPTIANS loved gardens, which they celebrated as places of beauty and romance. Verses from a 19th-dynasty (1293-1185 BC) papyrus include these lines sung by a woman in a garden:

I am your best beloved.
I am yours like this field which
    I have planted with flowers . . .
a lovely place for strolling,
with your hand in mine.
My body is satisfied, my heart
    in joy
at our going out together.
Hearing your voice is
    pomegranate wine;
I live for hearing it!

IN GREEN SHADE
A pool was the key feature in every Egyptian garden. The *shaduf*, a water-lifting device, made irrigation a good deal easier.

Gardens were laid out for temples, tombs and private houses, with brightly coloured flowers, trees for shade and a decorative pool which also provided water for irrigation. The lotus or water lily, a favourite flower, was charged with religious significance. The sun god, Atum, was said to have emerged from a lotus as a child. Indigenous species included the white *Nymphaea lotus* and the blue *Nymphaea caerula*. The pink-flowered Eastern sacred lotus, *Nelumbo nucifera*, was introduced from India during Persian times.

Gardens were first cultivated for food, and even at the cramped workmen's huts in el Amarna the villagers had small plots where they eked out their rations with home-grown vegetables. If they had no garden, people still grew flowers and shrubs in clay pots in the courtyard.

The larger gardens were enclosed by high walls. The owners walked among fig trees and date palms, and took their rest in shady arbours and vine-covered pergolas. The setting was idyllic; but in the blinding heat of an Egyptian summer, keeping plants well watered was a back-breaking chore. The text known as the *Satire on Trades* describes the life of a professional gardener as unenviable: 'And the gardener is bringing a yoke, each of his shoulders weighted with age and with a great swelling on his neck, which is festering; he spends the morning watering the corianders, and his supper is by the *Shaut*-plants, having spent midday in the orchard. Because of his produce, it happens that he sinks down dying, more so than with any other trade.'

and deposited it into a jar. (Rather than squander the water, the servants would probably have re-used it on the garden.)

The rich had lavatories that consisted of a wooden seat on brick supports with a pan half-filled with sand underneath. Even in the poorer homes there is likely to have been some sort of sanitary arrangement, even if it comprised no more than a sand-filled pot in a corner of the room. Herodotus contrasted the Egyptians' habits of eating in the open but relieving themselves indoors with customs in his own country (where people did things the other way round). Dung was not wasted. One of the jobs allocated to women and children was to gather up any stray human or animal droppings, mix them with straw and pat them into cakes. These were laid out on the roof to dry, and then used for fuel.

POTS, LAMPS AND LOCKS

Nile mud not only supplied Egypt with the material to make bricks – it also furnished the material for pots and jars to hold the housewife's stocks of water, wine, oil, milk and salted food. Potters turned their vessels on a low turntable that spun on a socketed stone base: the true potter's wheel, with a rotating mechanism operated by foot, was introduced in about 525 BC.

The pots themselves were utilitarian and unfussy in design. If more elaborate items were seen about the house they were generally foreign imports, originating in Minoan Crete, Cyprus or Syria. Nile clay was not of a particularly good quality, and was perhaps unsuitable for very fine pottery, although some fine work was produced, such as the 'medum ware' of the Old Kingdom, and the blue-painted wares of the New Kingdom. Most domestic pottery was used for cooking and storage, and probably did not last long, which accounts for its very ordinary appearance.

Other containers about the Egyptian house ranged from small glass pots, made in Egypt, for ointments and cosmetics to the large wooden storage chests which held the household linen. The Egyptians must have had their crime problems, for their houses were fitted with wooden doors locked by bolts. The bolts slid from the frame into a wooden block and were secured with pins. To seal a chest, the householder would lash the knobs on the lid and the side together using rope made from palm-leaf fibre or flax. A ball of mud might then be applied to the binding, and stamped with a seal impression. Of course, only the rich with treasures to protect would need such a device; indeed, the mere possession of a wooden chest implied a degree of prosperity, for timber was a scarce

AND SO TO BED . . .

THE BED was a considerable status symbol, distinguishing the sophisticated Egyptian from the peasant and 'sand-dweller' (the Bedouin). The framework was sprung with woven rush, and legs sometimes tapered down to carved animal hoofs or paws. Beds sloped somewhat towards the foot and often came equipped with a footboard – presumably to prevent the sleeper from slipping.

Instead of a pillow – uncomfortable on hot nights – people laid their head on a headrest. This was made from a piece of wood or stone curved to support the neck and occasionally wrapped in layers of cloth to make it less hard. Similar headrests are still used in parts of Africa today. In ancient Egypt, there were fancifully shaped headrests fashioned, for example, to resemble a crouching hare. Some were even carved with the owner's name and title – and with a prayer asking for a good night's sleep.

Linen bed coverings were stored in chests of wood or woven reed. A patterned rug might grace the bedroom floor, and there were portable commodes in case of urgent need during the night. The magic hippopotamus wand was a bedroom accessory designed to ward off any scorpions or snakes that might approach during the night. The wand was carved with images of protective deities from the ivory of the hippopotamus, one of the biggest and strongest animals known to the Egyptians. The wand was usually laid near the bed – and was possibly used to draw magic circles of protection around it – before people went to sleep.

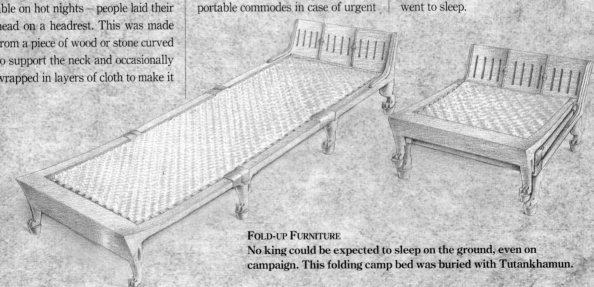

FOLD-UP FURNITURE
No king could be expected to sleep on the ground, even on campaign. This folding camp bed was buried with Tutankhamun.

KITCHEN SCENE Much cooking was done in Egypt on small braziers which could easily be set up in kitchen or courtyard, or even on the roof. Bread was often baked in a domed oven of moulded clay. Left: baskets were used for storing dry food.

commodity. After clay pots, baskets were the type of household container most commonly used. They were made either from plaited palm leaves or from grasses in stitched coil-work. Families lit their homes at night with shallow stone or pottery bowls containing castor oil and a wick made of twisted flax or papyrus. These simple lamps might be placed in wall niches or, in the wealthiest homes, positioned on shapely lamp stands made from painted wood. At dinner, ordinary folk squatted together around low wooden tables or built-in earthenware platforms. The modern type of dining table was not a feature in

Egyptian homes. At the workmen's settlement of Deir el-Medina, people ate around a raised platform in the main room of each home by day, and at night the owner of the house and his wife used the same platform for sleeping on. At the banquets of the rich, the guests sat round in little groups, and were served from small tables loaded with food and wine. There was no cutlery. Rich and poor alike ate with their fingers, scooping up food from a shared bowl. For the sake of cleanliness the Egyptians would pour water over each other's hands both before and after the meal.

For seating there were built-in earthenware benches and various types of stool, coming in fold-up, flare-legged and animal-footed types. The chair was a considerable status symbol, sometimes inlaid with ebony or ivory and strictly reserved for the elite. Similarly, while the great mass of the people slept at night on simple rush mats, the rich had fine wooden beds with headrests and blankets.

HANGING VASE A prehistoric cooking pot, shaped like a hedgehog, with handles by which it was suspended. Made of terracotta, it dates back to 4-3000 BC.

AN OFFICIAL HOMECOMING

THE HOUSEHOLD rejoices as its head comes home, bringing gifts from the pharaoh. The people of the Nile did business by barter, without any kind of cash currency. Wealth was distributed from above: by the pharaoh to his nobles, and by the nobles to the lower orders. This reward system was one way in which valuable commodities such as gold spread downwards through society.

The owner of this large town house is a high-ranking official at the court of the pharaoh. The main building stands in a central block, with an enclosing wall around it. The entrance courtyard to the left is approached by a guarded gateway. To the right lie the servants' quarters giving access to stables, cattle byres and storage areas for food. In the yard stand huge, beehive-shaped silos holding grain, which was essential for making the two staples of the household diet: bread and beer.

GARDEN

MAIN ENCL
WAL

MAIN ENTRANCE

GATE TO INNER
ENCLOSURE

ROAD TO
MAIN ENTRANCE

IN RECEPTION ROOM

OFFICIAL

WIFE

KITCHEN & SERVANTS' QUARTERS

GRAIN SILOS

CLOTHES AND COSMETICS

Cool white linen, the glimmer of colourful jewellery, elegant hairstyles

and flashing eyes dark with kohl . . . the ancient Egyptians created a look that remains

as alluring today as it did 4000 years ago.

MOST FAMILIES made their own clothes. Cloth was mainly made in temple and palace workshops, and was issued as rations to working people, although families did some weaving at home. Flax was combed and spun by a spindle whorl into thread of various weights, producing fabrics that ranged from the coarsest type of sackcloth to linen so fine it was almost transparent.

Though spinning and weaving were thought to be women's work, in some of the larger workshops in the towns fabrics were mass-produced by working men. These were dens of what later came to be described as

EGYPTIAN TUNIC   The garment is made of linen and wool, and dates from the 5th century AD.

sweated labour, and their produce was destined for the pharaoh, priests and nobles. According to a papyrus known as the *Satire on Trades*, 'the weaver in the workshop – he is worse than a woman. His knees are drawn up to his belly, he cannot breathe the open air. If he cuts short the day's weaving he is beaten with fifty thongs. He must give food to the doorkeeper that he lets him see the light of day'.

Clothing itself was simple, changing little over thousands of years except for a burst of stylistic innovation during the New Kingdom period (1570-1070 BC). A man's basic garment was a linen kilt made of a piece of cloth wrapped round the body and knotted at the waist. The Egyptians avoided unnecessary stitching, preferring to drape and knot (or fasten with a buckle) whenever possible. The impact of the desert sun influenced clothing as so much else in Egyptian culture. Garments had to be light, airy and uncomplicated, and people were not prudish about seeing bare flesh. Labourers often went about their

LINEN KILT   The chief item of menswear was a kilt, or simple apron knotted around the waist. The men in this fishing boat from a Theban tomb painting wear a typical triangular loin cloth.

work naked, or wore nothing more than a twist of linen around the loins. Upper-class Egyptians, too, seemed quite happy to go about in a loincloth in the privacy of their homes – though a flowing robe of white linen was customary for public appearances. And nobody bothered much about shoes. Even the wealthy seem to have been happy enough to pad barefoot about the house, though they would probably put on a pair of sandals when going out in public. The manufacture of sandals is shown in tomb paintings, and examples have survived. They are made of leather, neatly woven rushes or papyrus, with a thong passing between the big and second toes.

FIGURE-HUGGING DRESSES

Women wore a calf-length sheath dress, roughly hemmed and falling from shoulder level or breast. The examples shown in statues and Egyptian tomb paintings tend to be sleeveless and very tight around the figure. This, though, does not quite match the evidence of the garments which have survived. Some of the earliest pieces of intact clothing ever found are dresses recovered from Egyptian sites, and they are baggier than their counterparts in art. The figure-hugging style depicted by painters and sculptors owes a lot to artistic licence.

White linen was the convention for women's clothing and men's wear alike. Besides being light and cool in summer, linen also offered some warmth on cold nights. Wool was much less common – Egyptian sheep did not have thick fleeces, and there was some sort of religious taboo on the material. Nor was coloured cloth much worn, except in the royal household or among foreigners. The Egyptians delighted in pure, immaculate whiteness. 'They wear linen clothes which they make a special point of washing incessantly', wrote Herodotus. For a radiant finish they would starch and bleach their garments, and for ornament they used pleating. Some linen was virtually corrugated with narrow pleats, for which a special pleating implement was devised.

A fashion revolution occurred

FIGURES OF FASHION Women wore loose-fitting robes over tunics during the New Kingdom. The wide skirt and hip-hugging pleats sported by this nobleman (left) are in the New Kingdom style of about 1400 BC. Sandals (left, below) were the main type of footgear, though people often went barefoot.

HEAD COVER Egyptians of both sexes wore wigs for banquets and ceremonies. Wigs were usually made from human hair which was sometimes waxed so that it could be styled and set.

during the New Kingdom when pleating became fantastically intricate and fringing was all the rage. Rich men sported new types of garments such as cloaks, sashes, under-kilts and wide-sleeved tunics. Women, meanwhile, took to wearing elaborately fringed and pleated robes over their sheath dresses. But such showiness was untypical. On the whole, if an Egyptian wanted to cut a fine figure, he or she did so more through fashion accessories – wigs, cosmetics and jewellery – than through fancy articles of clothing.

WIGS AND COSMETICS

Egyptian men generally wore their hair cropped short or even shaved it off completely with a razor. This may have been done to combat the heat, but it also enabled men of the upper classes to put on imposing wigs for public occasions. Affluent women donned wigs too, though they normally wore them over their own hair. Styles for both sexes were often elaborately curled and plaited, and there were different styles for festive events and everyday use.

A CURE FOR BALDNESS

The Egyptians worried about hair loss, as other peoples have done throughout history. A hair restorer made for Queen Shesh, mother of King Teti, was concocted by boiling up the hoof of an ass, the stone of a date and the paw of a female greyhound. 'Apply liberally', read the instructions.

Egyptian wigs were made of human hair which was often bulked out with a plant fibre of some sort. One surviving example consists of about 120,000 individual hairs, grouped in 300 strands. Coated with a mixture of beeswax and resin, the hairs were looped through a netting and fixed in place with wax. The wig was then styled with a tumbling mass of blondish curls over a contrasting multitude of thin, tight plaits. Women further adorned their wigs and hairstyles with tassels, tiaras and beads, using pins and combs to hold curls in place. For a woman of fashion, preparing the hair must have been a time-consuming business, and the lady at her coiffure, aided by a servant or friend, formed a recurring motif for Egyptian artists and sculptors.

However many wigs people might possess, they still worried about grey hairs and bald patches. Hair tonics were varied and bizarre. Men smeared their heads with lion's fat as a cure for baldness, and to restore a rich black sheen to silver locks doctors suggested the blood of a black cow boiled in oil, the fat of black snakes and the contents of ravens' eggs. But while a good head of hair was thought enviable, facial hair was not admired – it reminded the Egyptians of foreigners and desert tribesmen. Also, many officials served in a priestly capacity at some time and needed to be 'pure' – which involved removing facial hair ... among other things. Men shaved regularly, although moustaches were

MIRROR IMAGE A polished bronze mirror of about 1300 BC. The handle is shaped in the image of a naked woman.

acceptable in the Old Kingdom, and beards were occasionally depicted by Egyptian artists. The Egyptians were using razors even before the time of the pharaohs, and by the New Kingdom a distinctive hatchet-shaped variety had evolved, with a sharp bronze blade fixed in a curved wooden handle. Soap, though, was unknown – the user presumably applied oil or an ointment to make shaving easier.

A mirror was essential for beauty treatment. Circular discs of polished copper were already in use during the reigns of the first pharaohs, and the Egyptians later made decorated bronze mirrors with handles, sometimes of ivory, shaped to resemble a nude woman, a papyrus column or the head of the goddess Hathor. Besides the pins and combs needed for keeping hair in place, there were tweezers for removing thorns, splinters or unwanted hair. Skin was smoothed with pumice stones and people used nail cleaners made from slivers of wood or bone. A 6th-dynasty tomb scene from Saqqara depicts a woman manicurist attending to her male client's right hand. In another she is dealing with his toenails. 'Don't hurt them!' the client pleads in a caption.

Egypt's hot sun and searing desert winds made moisturisers important for beauty care. Doctors suggested oil of fenugreek as a cure for wrinkles and freckles, and the fat of the cat, the crocodile and the hippopotamus as unguents.

Eye make-up had a long history in ancient Egypt: both men and women were painting eyelids and eyebrows as early as 4000 BC. Green and black were the favourite colours and the powders, ground on a palette, were mixed with water to form a paste, sometimes with an admixture of gum. The green paint had magical significance: it evoked the eye of the hawk-headed god Horus, and was sometimes painted right down from the eyebrow to the nose. Green was obtained from malachite, a copper ore imported from the Sinai desert, and it was more popular than black at the time when the pyramids were being built.

AN ALL-PURPOSE CLEANSER

The Egyptians did not possess bars of soap. When washing clothes, they used natron, a mixture of sodium carbonate and bicarbonate which dissolves grease, and is found in natural deposits in the desert. Natron was also used as a mouthwash. First thing in the morning, the health-conscious Egyptian would swill round teeth and gums with a little natron dissolved in water. This was the *sen shem shem* – 'cleansing of mouth and teeth'.

By the New Kingdom period, however, the black eye paint known as kohl had won favour. This was made from galena, a sulphide of lead which was mined particularly at Gebel el-Zeit in the eastern desert. Kohl created the compelling, almond-eyed look which is for most people the face of ancient Egypt. It was not only applied to add allure to the eyes, however: Egyptian physicians prescribed kohl against many eye diseases. Besides helping to shield the eyes from the sun, galena possesses disinfectant properties – and it also works as a fly deterrent.

Fashionable women often treated themselves to a mudpack of powdered alum. They reddened their hair and tinted their nails with henna, a dye obtained from the leaves and shoots of the henna shrub. To rouge their cheeks and lips, they might occasionally dab on some red ochre, and as an additional touch a lady of taste would put on perfume. The Egyptians were sensitive to bodily odours. Numerous perfumes were obtained from flowers, fruits and seeds whose fragrance was blended into a cream made from oil and animal fats. Wealthy women used scents based on the prized aromatic oil *balanos*, but castor oil was more common. Frankincense, myrrh, cinnamon, cardamom, sweet rush and bitter almonds were just a few of the other ingredients which mingled with one another to load the air with their fragrance.

'THE FLESH OF THE GODS'

Jewellery added the finishing touch to the outfits of wealthy Egyptians. Exquisite creations were produced especially under the 12th dynasty, a golden age of achievement in the arts.

The purpose of jewellery was partly magical. Many items took the form of amulets designed to ward off the evil eye and to protect the wearer against menacing forces, natural or supernatural. People wore charms fashioned in images of the gods or of animals, magical signs, hieroglyphs or the parts

MAKING EYES **A coffin portrait of the 18th-dynasty Queen Meryetamun shows her wearing kohl – the main cosmetic for eye make-up.**

BEAUTY TREATMENT FOR THE FASHION CONSCIOUS

DECORATED PERFUME boxes and cosmetic spoons are among the most exquisite articles produced in ancient Egypt. The artistry lavished on these small personal objects says as much for the people's delight in everyday life as the pyramids speak for their concerns with immortality.

The British Museum contains a fine example of an Egyptian make-up kit, discovered at Thebes and dating back to about 1300 BC in the New Kingdom period. The wooden chest is usually referred to as the cosmetics box of the Lady Tutu, wife of the scribe Ani, because it was found among his burial effects. In reality, though, it may have belonged to Ani himself, since Egyptians of both sexes used make-up. The chest is divided into four compartments holding jars and phials for creams and ointments. Here, too, were a small palette for mixing cosmetics and eye paint, a pumice stone for smoothing off unwanted hairs, and an elbow cushion on which to rest the arm during the long toilette. Perhaps the most delightful find was a pair of red boudoir slippers made of soft antelope leather.

During the New Kingdom, cosmetic spoons of wood, bone or ivory were often carved to resemble a swimming girl. The spoons were needed for perfumes as well as unguents, because perfume in ancient Egypt generally took the

A LADY'S TOILETTE A relief carving shows the 11th-dynasty Queen Kawit being beautified by her servants, one of whom adjusts her wig. Right: the cosmetics box of the Lady Tutu, dating from about 1300 BC.

form of a scented cream rather than a volatile liquid. Modern methods of steam distillation to extract essences were not known. Animal fats and vegetable oils formed the base, and fragrances were mingled using one of three methods. The first was enfleurage, by which aromatic flowers were embedded in layers of fat to lend them their aroma. The second was maceration, which involved pounding flowers, fruits or herbs in mortars and stirring the mixture into fats or oils heated to about 65°C (150°F). In the third method, flowers or seeds were gathered into a bag with a stick at each end. When the sticks were twisted, an aromatic juice was squeezed out, later to be mixed with fat or oil.

Putting on make-up, dabbing on scent, manicuring nails and arranging her elaborate hairstyle or wig made the morning toilet a wearisome business for an Egyptian woman of high fashion. One relief from the 11th dynasty (2023-1963 BC) shows Queen Kawit seated in an armchair, while a servant attends to her coiffure from behind. She raises a bowl of milk to her lips while a second servant fills another with liquid, saying: 'For your *ka* [spirit] my lady, take this drink I offer you.'

A Young Egyptian Princess

NEBTET SPENT the morning idling in the gardens of the great palace, where the sun cast razor-edged shadows across the ground. Beside one of the ornamental ponds she played with her little wooden crocodile, tugging at the string which made its jaw snap in the hope of startling the fishes that moved below the lotus leaves. Then she reached over the water's edge to pluck a pink flower, and she plaited it into the one long side lock hanging from the side of her head. Nebtet wore no clothes to speak of, but the sun glittered on her gold earrings and on her necklace of brilliant beads – turquoise, lapis and carnelian.

After some time she was joined at the pool by her younger sister, Nodjmet, and together they played catch with a leather ball, tossing it across the water, almost daring one another to let it fall in. And in the end it did – dropping with a splash into the pond, so that they had to call one of the gardeners to retrieve it for them. The man was a bearded Syrian, burnt black by the sun. He spoke not a word as he waded into the water and reached down to find the ball.

The princesses' nurse, Sechemt, who was picking figs nearby, now scolded the girls for disturbing the man at his work. So they moved away from the pool and went to play with their pet monkey in the dappled shade of a latticed pergola. At midday, when it became uncomfortably hot, their nurse called them into the palace where they joined the royal women for lunch. The girls squatted among heaps of brightly coloured cushions, dipping their hands into a bowl of cool water as servants brought cold plover, water melon, dates, honey and caraway cakes. The delicacies were laid out on low tables and the girls picked at them with deft fingers.

When the meal was over, Nebtet was scolded again by her nurse, this time for forgetting to wash her hands. Sticky fingers, she was told, would not please the gods – that afternoon they were to make offerings at the temple.

It was quite an occasion. Nebtet and her sister went in a palanquin with their father the great pharaoh, and their mother the queen. A host of palace guards and officials came with them. Out in the streets, Nebtet glimpsed people gaping in amazement at the procession: poor women in threadbare tunics; tradesmen at their workshop doors; girls little older than herself, carrying heavy wares on their heads. The princess and her sister were borne through a maze of paved courts to the doors of a splendid temple where servants piled the altar high with offerings of geese, fruit, flowers and vegetables. The girls enjoyed their own part in the ritual: they were clad now in flowing robes of pleated linen and were required to shake sacred rattles, known as *sistra*, while their parents tossed fragrant Arabian gums upon flaming vessels of bronze. But Nebtet could not fully understand the words intoned by the shaven-headed priests, and could not really see the point of all these appeals to the gods.

That night, before retiring to bed with her sister, Nebtet looked out on the dark palace garden. Moon-cast shadows played among the palms, and she imagined sinister forces moving about there: evil spirits as well as real-life crocodiles with real snapping jaws. Suddenly, she was very glad that they had made offerings at the temple that day. And before climbing into bed beside Nodjmet she offered up a prayer to the gods to keep them both safe from night perils.

SWIMMING GIRL Cosmetic spoons of this type represent the sky goddess Nut (the Milky Way) together with the constellation Cygnus.

of the body they were designed to keep safe. Precious stones were believed to possess magical potency, especially turquoise, carnelian and lapis lazuli. Gold, referred to as 'the flesh of the gods' was enormously significant. A lustrous metal which did not tarnish, it shone like the sun god – and was credited with the sun god's powers.

The Egyptians had access to the richest gold supplies in the ancient world, situated in the eastern desert and in Nubia to the south. Gold was crushed from veins of the desert's white quartz rock, and panned from the silt of *wadi*-beds. The nuggets and particles, tied in linen bags, were carried on donkey-back to the Nile valley. Much of it ended up in the workshops of the pharaoh or his priests, where skilled goldsmiths converted it into treasures for palace or temple. Sheet gold was hammered onto furniture and paper-thin gold leaf used to gild statues. The precious ore was also wrought into personal ornaments such as amulets, bangles, earrings and finger-rings.

In New Kingdom times, Egypt was famed throughout the eastern Mediterranean as a land where gold was very common. But silver was much rarer, coming chiefly from distant sources in Asia, and it was more highly prized than gold. Jewellers also made ornaments from electrum, a natural alloy of gold and silver. They drilled, polished, chased and engraved. They were skilled, too, at repoussé, or relief moulding, as well as cloisonné – different coloured semiprecious stones separated by thin metal strips.

One of the most distinctive Egyptian accessories was the bead collar worn around the neck, and which were sometimes wide enough to cover most of the chest. The beads were made from semi-precious stones, and splendid effects could be achieved through patterning with different colours of bead, strung in rows. Hair done, made up and perfumed, with bracelets and anklets chinking as they walked, Egyptian men and women of high fashion must have presented an elegant sight as they went out in public or to dine with friends at night.

JEWELLED DELIGHTS
The necklace of beads was for everyday wear. Guests at banquets wore collars of similar beads, with garlands of flowers. Below: a protective Eye of Horus amulet.

COLLARS AND PECTORALS Besides fantastic headgear, the royal beauty above wears a broad beaded collar – one of the most distinctive forms of adornment in Egypt. Left: a pectoral, or chest ornament, from the tomb of Tutankhamun. It takes the form of a scarab, or sacred dung beetle.

FOOD AND DRINK

Pelicans' eggs, stewed antelope and pomegranate wine were just a few of the delicacies

which graced the tables of Egypt's elite. Poorer folk survived on much plainer fare.

Yet the people as a whole were well fed.

T O THE DESERT PEOPLES who lived east and west of Egypt, the civilisation of the Nile was a gourmet's paradise. 'Think of it!' complained the hungry Israelites travelling in the wilderness after the Biblical Exodus, 'In Egypt we had fish for the asking, cucumbers and watermelons, leeks and onions and garlic.' Indeed, the fields bordering the great river, the groves of fruit trees all yielded a wealth of foodstuffs.

Most of Egypt's fertile acreage, however, was given over to the growing of grain – and specifically to the grains barley and wheat. These in their turn provided the two main staples of the Egyptian diet: bread and beer. At the lower levels of society, families survived, day in, day out, on precious little else. Housewives always made their own bread, grinding the corn on a saddle stone (a block of stone with a central depression) to make the flour. Then they mixed the flour with

KITCHEN STAFF Household servants prepare the bread and brew the beer in a domestic scene from the 12th dynasty.

water and kneaded it into a smooth dough to make the bread.

An oven-baked flat loaf, resembling modern Greek pitta bread, was common in ancient Egypt, and similar loaves are still eaten by Egyptians to this day. Another popular loaf was conical: it was made in a mould and then baked over an open fire. But there were fancier shapes, too: triangular loaves, for example, ovals and indented squares, as well as loaves in the form of animals and human figures. The luxury items were exotically flavoured with palm nuts, or sometimes sweetened with honey or dates.

Much Egyptian bread was coarse and gritty, which accounts for the unusually worn-down condition of the teeth of Egyptian mummies. In many cases, dental attrition was so bad that teeth were reduced to no more than stumps level with the gums, as X-rays have shown. The impurities may

HEAVY DUTY Well-laden porters brought food and drink to the rich man's house in baskets, rushwork sacks, pottery jars or stoneware containers.

have come from certain types of quern stone that were used in the grinding of the grain, but they may also have derived from wind-blown sand at almost any stage of production. Certainly, the evidence of wear and abcesses is such that toothache must have plagued Egyptians of all classes.

Everyone drank beer – it was even brought by mothers to their children at school. The drink was made at home from a barley loaf, which was lightly baked to activate the yeast without killing it. Mashed and then mixed with water, the concoction fermented to create a soupy brew which was later sieved and decanted into jars. To give taste and body, dates or various other

---

EYEWITNESS

HABITS OF THE MARSH PEOPLE

THE GREEK HISTORIAN Herodotus was born between 490 and 480 BC, and travelled widely in Egypt. He described a number of the customs of the marshy delta, including those of lotus-eating and the use of mosquito nets:

❝ The people of the marshes gather the water lilies (called lotus by the Egyptians) which grow in masses when the river is swollen and spills over the neighbouring flatlands. They dry the plants in the sun and then, from the centre of each blossom, they pick out something which looks like a poppy-head. This they grind and make into loaves which they bake. The root of the plant is

also edible; it is round, about the size of an apple, and tastes sweet . . . They also harvest the annual crop of papyrus reed, cut the stalks in two and eat the lower part, which is about 18 inches in length. To enjoy this delicacy to perfection, they first bake it in a sealed pan which is heated red hot . . .

The Egyptians who live in the marsh country use an oil extracted from the castor-oil plant. This plant, which grows wild in Greece, they call *Kiki*. The Egyptian variety is very prolific and has an unpleasant smell. Their practice is to sow it along the banks of rivers and lakes, and when the fruit is gathered it is

either bruised and pressed, or else it is boiled down. The resulting oil is just as good as olive oil for burning in lamps, though the smell is still unpleasant.

The country is infested with swarms of mosquitoes . . . [Everyone] in the marsh country equips himself with a net which he uses for fishing during the day. At night he fixes it up round his bed and then he creeps in under it before going to sleep. It would be hopeless to try and sleep wrapped up in a cloak or in linen cloth, for the mosquitoes would just bite through them. ❞

From *The Histories* by Herodotus

flavourings might be added. Most Egyptian beer had an alcoholic content of about 8 per cent, though beers of different strengths were also prepared, and their potency was indicated by the colour on the container. Red was the standard strength; black the most potent. Wealthy connoisseurs drank imported beers from Syria. Beer had strong religious associations, and was distributed in colossal quantities to pilgrims at Dendera, during the annual festival of Hathor, the goddess of fertility.

The typical Egyptian workman's wife would often add an onion, a leek or a cucumber to her husband's packed lunch of bread and beer. Onions, in particular, were relished by the ancient Egyptians and, eaten with bread, they formed the only luxury in many a poor man's daily diet. Eye-watering fare it might seem – but these ancient onions are thought to have been a good deal sweeter than their modern counterparts, and therefore less prone to make the eyes smart. They were smaller, too, than the modern ones, and had round white bulbs with long green stems, rather like our own spring onions.

The Roman writer Juvenal (*c.* AD 60-130) was to mock Egypt as a country where, 'onions are adored and leeks are gods'. Melons, gourds, radishes, garlic and lettuces (elongated varieties, like the modern cos type) all offered further variety to the basic cereal diet. People gathered wild celery for the table, and the all-purpose papyrus provided food, prepared from its roasted root. Many meals must have consisted only of pulses: peas, beans, chick peas and lentils. By examining the stomach contents of bodies dating back to 3150 BC, the experts have discovered that lentils were being cultivated in Egypt long before the pharaohs' time.

FAVOURED FRUIT A hand reaches for a fig in this detail from a 19th-dynasty wall painting. Figs were not only eaten fresh, but used as sweeteners in cooking.

THE PERILS OF PORK

Pig meat may first have been shunned as unclean because it is prone to harbour parasites. Medical analysis of Egyptian mummies has revealed evidence of *trichinella* cysts resulting from parasites found in undercooked, infected pork.

The few trees that flourished in Egypt's arid climate were highly prized: the dom-palm, for example, bearing gingery-tasting nuts, the sycamore fig and the persea tree (*Mimusops schimperi*) bearing apple-flavoured fruit. The dry-tasting Egyptian plum (*Cordia myxa*) was also savoured, as was the mandrake whose slightly toxic fruit was sniffed at banquets for its narcotic effect. Dates, pomegranates, figs and plums, all provided their different liqueurs and wines, as well as fruit for the table.

The vine was cultivated in Egypt as well. The art of wine-making seems first to have been developed in Asia Minor. It then spread south to Egypt, where wealthy people acquired connoisseur tastes. They enjoyed red and white varieties, both sweet and dry. Wine jars, sealed with clay, were labelled with full details of the type, the vineyard and the year of the vintage. The best wine was produced from the juice of the first pressing, when workers trod the grapes in an open tank, as port treaders do today in Portugal. Unlike their Portuguese counterparts who link arms with one another, however, the Egyptian workers steadied themselves by holding onto bars just above head height, which were set up above the treading floor. A lower-grade wine was obtained by gathering up the pulped grapes, pips and stems in a giant sack

GRAPE PICKERS Vines were trained up trellises and espaliers, as well as being grown as small bushes. The Egyptians preferred dark-skinned grapes.

must have lent its own taste to the drink, much like *retsina*, the resin-flavoured wine of modern Greece.

Still, the Egyptian connoisseur must have been looking for other qualities in wines than those recognised by his counterpart today. For the art of wine-making was keenly pursued and makers evidently found ways of letting good wines mature without turning vinegary. What other reason was there for recording the year of the vintage? When the tomb of Tutankhamun was opened, 36 wine jars were found among the grave goods, many of them labelled with a date. Altogether, wine-making had considerable mystique: not for nothing did the pharaoh's palace manager style himself the 'bearer of the secrets of the wine-hall'.

which was then twisted with wooden poles to squeeze out what was left.

Wine was always a rich man's drink in Egypt, and discriminating noblemen particularly admired the wines that were imported from the land of Canaan (modern Israel and Jordan). Egypt's own best vineyards were reckoned to be grouped to the west of the Nile delta, at Memphis, Sile, Behbeit el-Hagar and oases in the Libyan desert. Egyptian wines, however, cannot have been of top quality, since they had to be sieved when poured out. Resin, too, was added as a preservative, and this

MILKING SCENE Cows were kept for breeding and for milk. The mother shown here is weeping. Most cattle were pastured in the swampy lands of the Nile delta.

BUTCHERS' WORK Cattle had their legs bound before being slaughtered. When the throat was slit, the blood was caught in a bowl and boiled to make a kind of black pudding.

Milk was drunk in ancient Egypt, and the people also made butter, cheese and curds. Dairy products such as these featured particularly in the diet of herdsmen; the protein they provided was especially valuable because meat was a luxury for most Egyptians. Though huge cattle herds were raised, few peasants would ever have tasted beef, which was destined for the tables of the nobility or for temple sacrifice. A haunch or leg of beef was a favourite offering in sacred ritual. After making the offerings the animal was jointed and formed part of the 'wages' of the priest. Archives from the temple of Raneferef at Abusir describe 130 bulls being sacrificed there in the space of just ten days.

If working people did get a chance to eat meat, it was more likely to be mutton or goat. And although eating pork was thought abhorrent to the gods, because pigs are omnivorous and therefore unclean, the number of pig bones found at some sites suggests that it

PAIN AND PLENTY The hunger shows in this Middle Kingdom figure of an emaciated man holding a bowl. But in times of plenty, rich Egyptians enjoyed a varied diet. Below: geese are herded and caged on a great estate.

COOKING IN EGYPT

ENTICING AROMAS drifted through the streets of Egyptian towns at mealtimes. Most families cooked in the open, so that the evening air was spiced with cumin, marjoram, garlic, coriander and dill. The smoke from skewered fish and wildfowl – both popular dishes – must have been tantalising to the poorest Egyptians, living on bread and onions.

Stoves and braziers were sited in courtyards and on roofs, and in a land where timber was scarce, the small branches of tamarisk and acacia were valued as fuel. Otherwise, people burned papyrus stalks, palm leaves or dried animal dung. Housewives lit their fires with a bow drill and a wooden block, and when sparks ignited the kindling, they fanned flames with a palm or papyrus fan. Once the fire was going, women fried their food in a wok-like clay pan with loop handles, or made stews in straight-sided pots. Most vessels were of unglazed clay, though the wealthier households had copper and bronze wares. The rich also had metal knives for chopping

and scraping while the poor used flint blades.

The basic peasant diet was vegetarian, and although no recipes have survived from ancient Egypt some traditional dishes that are still enjoyed today may date back to the time of the pharaohs. One of these is *felafel*. It consists of fried rissoles, made of mashed beans mixed with garlic, onions and spices, and it is a classic dish of the Copts (who are the descendants of the ancient Egyptians). Certainly, the ingredients were all available under the pharaohs.

Once in a while – especially at festival times – even humble folk might enjoy a taste of meat in the form of a spit-roasted duck or a pigeon served split in half, flattened and grilled. For the nobles, there was much richer fare: goodly joints of beef, pelican eggs, pomegranate, date or grape wine and fancily prepared honeycakes. Geese were force-fed with pellets of

FATTENING CRANES A 5th-dynasty tomb scene shows cranes being force-fed for the table.

sweetened bread moistened with oil or wine. And lords returning from hunting expeditions at the desert's edge brought back antelopes and gazelles for the stewing pot.

---

also played some part in the labourer's diet. When livestock was slaughtered, nothing was wasted: soups and stews were made by boiling up the bones, and fat was rendered down for cooking purposes. Among the ruins of a palace of Amenophis III, archaeologists have found jars containing the remnants of fat from goat, beef and mutton. In present-day Egypt a fat known as *alya* is obtained by rendering a sheep's tail, and it may have been by this method that the poor got most of their cooking fat in ancient times.

The reedbeds of the Nile teemed with birds, from ducks and geese to herons, ibises, cranes, cormorants

ROOSTER A sketch of a cockerel. Domestic fowl like this did not become common in Egypt until the Roman period.

and flamingos. Professional wildfowlers sometimes caught them in traps or draw nets, in order to fatten them up over winter. Roast goose was often eaten at the time of the great religious festivals.

Chickens, originally from Southeast Asia, had reached Egypt by the 14th century, presumably through trading contacts with the Near East. A handsome cockerel is represented on a sherd, or piece of broken pottery, in the Valley of the Kings. But chickens were only farmed in Egypt in any numbers during Roman times. For eggs, the Egyptians relied chiefly on ducks and geese, as well as on birds less familiar to modern Western man – such as pelicans.

GONE FISHING The Nile thronged with fish, and though their flesh is said to have been taboo for priests it played an important part in the national diet. Fishermen are often depicted in noblemen's tombs such as this one from Saqqara.

The occasional pigeon provided ordinary people with a further source of protein, and fish was also important. The Nile teemed with fish, which were grilled on long skewers or boiled in cauldrons to make stews. Quantities of fish were preserved by salting or pickling, and more were dried in the sun, wrapped in the ashes of burnt grass. The gangs of artisans who dug out and decorated the royal tombs at Thebes had fishermen attached to them, providing 40lb (18 kg) of fish every ten days. Priests abstained from eating fish because various species were held sacred – especially the Nile perch, on which a whole cult was centred.

A CURIOUS USE FOR ONIONS

The onion – Egypt's favourite vegetable – was remarkably adaptable. When archaeologists examined the mummy of Ramses IV they found two small onions serving as artificial eyeballs in the skull. New Kingdom embalmers often put something in the sockets to lend a lifelike curve to the eyelids. Artificial eyeballs were usually of stone, but onions in this case provided a perfectly serviceable substitute.

Oil was a vital commodity in every household, used not only for cooking but also for lighting, cosmetic ointments and medicine. One common cooking oil was derived from sesame seed, but there were other sources, too, including the fruits of the balanos and moringa trees, as well as linseed and the seed of the castor-oil plant. Olive oil was imported in large quantities from Palestine.

Salt was another essential, found in the homes of rich and poor alike. The temples are known to have employed people as salt gatherers, and salt was often used in barter. The main sources were natural deposits in the desert and oases, but it was also obtained by panning on the sea coast.

Honey was the all-purpose sweetener. It came from the flower-spangled meadows bordering the Nile where cone-shaped beehives of dried mud produced a red variety, as well as a clear honey obtained by heating and straining the wax. Both were expensive, however, and studies of Egyptian teeth suggest that honey cannot have been consumed in any great volume. While serious dental abrasion resulted from crunching on gritty bread, the people seem to have been free of the decay which afflicts modern Western men and women as a result of eating sugary foods.

EGYPTIAN TOWNS AND TRADES

'Cause a cow-hide or a goat-hide to be brought and give it to Wereniptah. Also, enter it in writing', runs a routine order from a sandal-maker, found in a 12th-dynasty temple archive. The Egyptians possessed neither money nor markets as we know them, so that every important exchange of goods had to be brought to the attention of scribes. With all transactions, diligent figures, like the ones depicted on the 18th-dynasty basrelief above, were needed to 'enter it in writing'.

LIFE IN THE CITY

Gigantic temples and palaces dominated the skylines of Egyptian cities.

Clustered around their walls were flat-roofed, mud-brick dwellings, lining mazes of streets

and courts where heaps of household refuse rotted on the ground.

EARLY IN THE MORNING, files of women balancing large jars on their heads passed through the streets of Egyptian towns and villages. They were fetching water – for drinking, cooking and washing. Ancient Egypt possessed no piped supplies, and although wells were dug, most of the water people used in their homes came from the Nile or from one of the pools and canals fed by the great river.

The water then had to be brought home and emptied into the large ceramic jars that stood by the front door or in the courtyard of private dwellings. Although the Nile's waters were the lifeblood of Egyptian civilisation, they were not entirely clean. The remains of various river-borne parasites have been discovered in Egyptian mummies, having invaded their victims either when they drank the water or waded through it. The virulent bilharzia

worm was among them – a cause of anaemia, inflammation, dysentery, debilitation and other disorders.

Towns grew up at regular intervals along the Nile and generally evolved in haphazard fashion, with a core of public buildings at the centre. Markets as we know them today did not exist, but a few tomb scenes show the barter of goods and provisions near the quays, for besides providing water for homes, the Nile also brought the great ships loaded with corn, wine, oil and quarried stone. Goods were traded, for money had not yet been invented.

Towns were often walled for protection against attack and against the devastating flood waters of the high Nile. The temples and palaces themselves were also enclosed by massive mud-brick walls, sometimes towering up to 50 ft (15 m) high and dominating the clustered houses of the workers. It seems that the royal palaces, also built largely of mud-brick, were often renewed and sometimes re-sited, so the centres of the major cities tended to move. Memphis, which was founded around 3100 BC, was the most important city until Alexandria became the capital of the Ptolemaic dynasty in about 300 BC.

WOODWORK
An Egyptian tomb model shows carpenters in their workshop. Most timber was imported.

MEAN STREETS
Dogs pick at the garbage in the streets. Waste disposal was always a problem.

Whilst its religious centre focused on the great stone-built temples, its administrative centre moved at different periods, resulting in a cluster of villages and settlements stretching for about 8 miles (12 km) from north to south. The pyramids, the sphinx at Giza and the cemetery at Saqqara were all part of the vast complex of monuments centred on the metropolis.

The streets of Memphis and other Egyptian towns were not made to accommodate wheeled traffic. Donkeys carried the heavier goods, and wealthy Egyptians passed by in swaying palanquins – carrying chairs borne high on the shoulders of pole-bearers. These must have been a blessing with the

amount of household refuse in the streets. Townsfolk swept everything out of their homes: broken pots, dirty rags, worn-out sandals, heaps of soot, piles of ash, builders' rubble, decomposing vegetable waste and animal bones. The rubbish mounds became a changeless feature of the urban scene in Egypt. Dogs, hyenas and vultures scavenged daily in the refuse, which also harboured the black rat, host to a flea that carries *Pasteurella pestis* – the bubonic plague.

People tried alternative means to dispose of their waste, tipping it into holes in the ground, into empty houses, and into the Nile and canals leading off it. Occasionally, piles of dried rubbish might be burned outside the town walls, but most garbage simply accumulated in the waste heaps. Outside the city walls of Akhetaten, archaeologists discovered a belt of official garbage mounds containing fragments of Aegean pottery, valuable glassware and items marked with royal names – waste from the nearby royal palace at Amarna and the great houses around it.

'MUST BE SEEN'

Akhetaten has provided an unusually detailed picture of a large-scale Egyptian settlement. The town was built by Akhenaten, the 18th-dynasty pharaoh, to be a

BRICKMAKERS **The Nile's banks furnished Egypt with plentiful mud for the mass production of bricks.**

QUAYSIDE COMMERCE **The great towns of Egypt were strung out along the Nile, and goods carried by river were bartered on the quayside.**

city of royal residence, and its name meant 'horizon of the Aten', referring to the cult that the pharaoh was trying to establish (the Aten was the radiant sun disc). Constructed at a virgin site on the Nile's east bank,

the city was intended for a long and splendid future, and great ceremony marked its opening. In the limestone cliffs on both sides of the Nile, sculptors chiselled 14 boundary markers, all decorated with

LIFE WITHOUT MONEY

COINED MONEY did not exist in ancient Egypt, nor was there a substantial class of middlemen who could be called merchants. Most people farmed the land and the state took the bulk of their produce, doling some of it out later to artisans, soldiers, workmen and slaves. Nonetheless, the basic system was augmented by a lot of bartering and haggling. People swapped grain for necklaces, pigs for wooden chests, and so on. For measuring quantities, the Egyptians used stone and metal weights, and late in the New Kingdom period, a

metal standard became fairly widely used. The weight of a metal was expressed in units that were known as *deben* (roughly 3 oz/85 g), each consisting of ten units known as *kite*. Thus a scale of values evolved although no money was in circulation.

For everyday purposes the main metal was copper, obtained from surface deposits in the valleys of western Sinai. A copper *deben* was rated at 100th of the value of a silver *deben*. Since it had to be imported from sources in Asia, silver was exceptionally scarce in ancient Egypt, and more highly prized than

gold throughout the time of the pharaohs. From the study of various prices originating from Deir el-Medina in the age of the Ramses kings, it has been possible to compare some prices:

1 sheep or goat = 1-3 copper *deben*
1 ass = 25-40
1 head of cattle = 20-150
1 chair = 12-30
1 table = 15
1 casket = 0.5-10
1 pair sandals = 0.5-3
1 leather bag = 0.5-3
1 razor = 1-2

images of the royal family. Before building began, the pharaoh toured the new city's outer limits. At every boundary marker he swore an oath dedicating himself to the sacred city, and vowing that when he died he would be buried there.

Akhetaten was laid out with temples of the sun, extensive royal buildings and a planned residential area for the affluent families. The rich lived in villas set in walled grounds, while retainers and dependants inhabited smaller houses grouped around. The compounds of the great officials were settled on a grid plan, with space for the smaller houses of their dependants and subordinates to grow around them. However, the village built for tomb workers towards the hills was different. This was laid out according to a rigid grid, with barrack-like housing blocks running along ruler-straight streets. There were 72 dwellings of uniform size and one larger overseer's house, all enclosed by a square wall. The village possessed no well, and water had to be brought from the river (about $1\frac{1}{2}$ miles (2 km) away) and stored in a guarded tank for distribution to the inhabitants.

Akhetaten stretched along the edge of the river, backed by a vast semicircular desert plain enclosed by cliffs. On the opposite (west) bank of the river, a corresponding area of rich agricultural land was allocated to the estates of the temples and officials of the town. When Akhenaten died, his dream died with him. Partly because of its location far south of Memphis and the other main centres, the city was abandoned after little more than 12 years of occupation, and its fallen palaces, temples, homes and workshops were to lie almost undisturbed under their barren plain until modern times.

They have proved a paradise for archaeologists. It was here, for example, that a German team discovered a painted limestone bust of the pharaoh's queen, Nefertiti, that has become the most famous single artefact surviving from ancient Egypt. Supremely elegant, with a slender neck and serene features, she was discovered in December 1912. The expedition's leader, Ludwig Borchardt, found himself at a loss for words when listing the objects he had found. 'I wrote', he said later, '"Description futile: Must be seen".'

LICK OF COLOUR Wildlife scenes graced palace walls. This is from Malqata, royal residence of Amenophis III.

LOST CITY, FORGOTTEN PHARAOH

IN 1887, AN EGYPTIAN woman from a village near the present-day site of el Amarna made an extraordinary discovery. She was digging for *sebakh*, a compost rich in nitrogen which is formed from the decay of ancient mud bricks. And in the course of her excavations, she came upon a cache of over 300 small clay tablets, imprinted with the wedge-shaped cuneiform script used by the peoples of ancient Mesopotamia and western Asia. The language was Akkadian, a tongue widely used in diplomacy, and the cache turned out to consist of correspondence sent to Egypt's pharaoh by vassal kings of Palestine and Syria. During a century of excavation, archaeologists have uncovered the ruins of temples and palaces whose walls once shone with coloured glass and stone: red quartzite, obsidian and black granite. This was Akhetaten, the royal capital founded by Egypt's strangest king, Akhenaten.

The pharaoh, who began his reign under the name of Amenophis IV, launched an astonishing episode in Egyptian history in 1357 BC, when he abandoned the worship of Amun-Re of Thebes and replaced it with the cult of a single deity, the Aten, which is the visible disc of the sun. The king changed his name to Akhenaten ('pleasing to the Aten') and moved his court to the virgin site at el Amarna 250 miles down the Nile from the city of Thebes.

The revolution in religion was matched by a new approach to art, which became more mannerist. Akhenaten himself was always depicted with thick lips, a curiously elongated head, rounded hips and a protruding stomach. These images suggested to Egyptologists that the king may have suffered from a glandular disorder, and doctors have suggested Frohlich's syndrome, which results from a malfunction of the pituitary gland or of the mesencephalon (the middle section of the brain). The odd-looking monarch and his queen, Nefertiti, often appear in intimate domestic scenes, bestowing kisses on their daughters or dangling them on their knees. Such images suggested an idyllic existence, and early Egyptologists tended to take a rather romantic view of the pharaoh and his religion, which they saw as the first monotheism. Similarities between the king's hymn to the sun and the Psalms suggested that Akhenaten was the pharaoh whom the Biblical Joseph served. Today, these ideas are mostly rejected by Egyptologists, and many scholars view Akhenaten as more reactionary than radical, trying to reinstate the sun-cult and autocratic kingship of the pyramid age.

Following Akhenaten's death (*c.*1340 BC), the worship of Amun-Re was restored and Akhetaten was soon abandoned, its temples pulled down and the stone re-used elsewhere. Akhenaten's name (and those of his successors, Tutankhamun and Ay) was omitted from the official lists of Egypt's pharaohs. If reference to his existence could not be avoided, allusion was made to the 'era of the rebel'. Akhenaten became a 'forgotten' pharaoh, as lost to history as the city that lay buried under Egypt's shifting sands.

RENEGADE KING **Akhenaten makes offerings to the sun – the deity he favoured over all the ancient gods.**

PLANNED TOWN

EGYPT'S MAIN URBAN centres grew up along the Nile, and they were walled as much for protection from flooding as from attack. To the left stands the temple enclosure, with its main building, subsidiary temple and sacred lake. Incorporating store-rooms, workshops and living quarters for the priests, it dominated the town. Yet only the outer parts – such as the shrine on the outer wall – were open to the public.

Some areas of towns were laid out on a grid plan, but their symmetry broke down with rebuilding works, and levels became irregular as new houses were built on the rubble of old.

Quays and harbours were built for unloading produce from river boats, and as ceremonial sites. The waterside thronged with crowds during religious festivals when, in some towns, the statue of the presiding local god, hidden for much of the year, was put on public display.

MAIN TEMPLE

SACRED LAKE

QUAYS

PROCESSIONAL WAY

PALACE

PRIESTS' HOUSES

STOREROOMS

WORKSHOPS

MEN AT WORK

Splendid statuary, elegant furniture, fine linen and glimmering jewellery –

all were the products of hard-working craftsmen toiling for Egypt's elite.

The most esteemed workers were well rewarded – others were treated as serfs.

THE FAMOUS HEAD of Nefertiti was discovered when archaeologists were exploring the workshop of a sculptor named Thutmose. Several more images of the queen were also found at the site, along with other portrait studies of the royal family. Thutmose was clearly a respected figure, because he had been given a smart new house with a master bedroom, bathroom, studios and quarters for his assistants. But in Egypt, artists were not thought of as grand or heroic figures – men set apart from society – but as skilled workers, no different from the goldsmiths, the furniture-makers and the jewellers who were also employed by the elite. Our modern fondness for novelty and creative invention was not shared in ancient Egypt. There, the artists' aim was to do the right thing in the right way, just as it had been done by their forefathers for centuries.

The sculptor used the same tools as the stonemason and (when working in soft limestone) the carpenter. As a portraitist, his job was to produce, with hammer and chisel, a likeness of his various subjects that smoothed out the blemishes, representing facial features at an ideal age of youth or full maturity. To help achieve a

REGAL SILHOUETTE
Nefertiti's features,
carved in quartzite.
The crown shown
in the bust
(now in Berlin) was
detachable.

likeness, sculptors took plaster casts both from the living and the dead, and a unique collection of these masks was found in Thutmose's studio, showing startlingly natural faces that are free from all stylisation.

Craftsmen like Thutmose were key figures in urban life, for Egypt's booming food production freed large numbers of people to do non-agricultural work. The busy workshops situated in every sizable town housed potters, stonemasons, carpenters, cabinet-makers, jewellers, metalworkers, glassworkers, weavers, tanners and a host of other tradesmen. Their tools as well as their workshops were the property of the palace, temple or nobleman who employed them, and there were no guilds as in medieval Europe to bond men working in the same trade. However, artisans did serve long apprenticeships, and at the end had to present a qualifying work as proof of their competence, like the 'master piece' required of an apprentice in the Middle Ages.

Specialist skills were first developed by artisans manufacturing their wares in their workshop homes. But already, under the Old Kingdom, factory production was well under way, as numbers of different craftsmen pooled their skills in order to make high-quality products for the pharaoh, the temples or the nobility. Mass-produced goods flooded out of the big workshops, and technology improved as artisans concentrated their minds on the various technical problems caused by different stages of

POWDER PAINTS Lumps of coloured pigment were ground down to make artists' paints. They were applied with brushes of the type shown on the right.

production. Stone-cutters, for example, devised a drill for boring holes in beads and stone vessels. It had a handle at the top, a wooden spindle and a sharpened stone or copper bit, with a weighted apparatus that saved the operator from the need to press down on the object as he drilled. Egyptian cabinetmakers perfected the art of dovetailing pieces of wood and jointing with dowels; and metalworkers discovered the *cire perdu* (lost wax) method of casting

objects in metal, by which a carved wax image is used to make a plaster mould and then melted away to leave a cavity into which the molten metal is poured.

'HE STINKS MORE THAN FISH-ROE'

Elegant though their products might be, many trades were hazardous to health. For example, before the Egyptians invented bellows in the New Kingdom, metalworkers used blowpipes to boost the heat of their fires. Their eyes must have suffered from glare and they were prone to emphysema (the swelling of air sacs in the lungs) resulting from the back-pressure caused by blowing down blowpipes for long periods of time. There was also the constant risk of bad burns. The miseries of metalworking are described in a document known as the *Satire on Trades*, in which a bureaucrat named Khety advises his son to become a scribe by cataloguing the misfortunes known to other tradesmen. Obviously the

SCULPTOR'S WORKSHOP Egyptian sculptors took plaster casts of their subjects to help achieve an accurate likeness.

How Glass was Made

NO ONE KNOWS who first stumbled on the secret of making glass, but the event seems to have happened somewhere in the Middle East – probably on a beach or in the desert, where a fire was lit and gleaming droplets of glass were later found shining in the sand. Glass is a composite of sand, limestone and soda fused at a high temperature; and the first pieces are likely to have been accidents.

In Egypt, the oldest examples are found in faience, a type of fine ware made by coating a core of sand and clay (or of stone) with a layer of glaze – glass and glaze were basically the same material. The Egyptians were manufacturing faience from about 4000 BC and came to excel at beads, amulets, statuettes and vessels.

In the first stage of glass-making the sand, limestone and soda were mixed together in a clay crucible. For a greenish or bluish effect, the makers would add a copper compound, while dark blue was formed using cobalt compounds; a milky-white hue was achieved with tin or lead oxide; and red and orange were created with copper oxides. The entire mixture was then heated to as much as 1100°C (2010°F) until its components fused in a single, molten mass. Any object dunked into the crucible would end up covered with a glaze.

The manufacture of pure glass vessels began in the New Kingdom as the Egyptians learned to take the cooled object and chip out its clay core, leaving the glaze, or glass coating, intact.

Glass-makers used a metal rod to dip the clay core into the molten mass, and they would then give the rod a few swift twists to spread the glass evenly. To decorate a vase, glassworkers often wound thin rods of coloured glass around the hot, glaze-covered core. The cold rods softened on contact and merged into its surface in parallel bands of colour. By drawing a sharp metal implement up and down the various coloured bands, the makers produced wavy or feathery patterns or patterns based on garlands of leaves and flowers. Feet and a rim were formed at the end of the process, and a handle could be added if necessary.

Under the pharaohs, glass-making was a royal monopoly. Glass was a luxury product and glass items were small: eye-paint containers, cosmetic jars and scent bottles. Most glass was tinted and opaque rather than transparent. The revolutionary technique of glass-blowing arrived at some time in the 1st century BC, probably from Syria – well known as a major centre of glassworking. Clear glass then became the rule, and output increased to the extent that glass lost something of its elite status.

LIFE OF TOIL Stonemasons are shown hard at work in this 18th-dynasty relief fragment. Left: A carpenter with his adze squats on a scaffolding platform. Untypically, he is shown scruffy and unshaven.

father was laying it on thick, but the text nonetheless provides vivid vignettes of working life's grimier and more off-putting aspects:

I have seen the metalworker at his labour
at the mouth of his furnace,
his fingers like the hide of a crocodile;
he stinks more than fish-roe.

Khety described the horrors known to weavers working under brutal overseers in dingy workshops. He spoke of the laundryman dealing with filthy linen – and crocodiles – on the riverbank. He wrote about potters grubbing like pigs in the mud, and about the monotony of life for the jeweller crouched all day over his stones: 'By the time he has finished an inlay he is tired and weak. He has to sit with his legs folded and back bent until sunset.' Life could evidently be hard for the Egyptian craftsmen.

Conditions, at least in the more esteemed trades, were by no means all bad. At Deir el-Medina, the architects and stonemasons employed to build royal tombs were provided with their own servants, as well as teams of women slaves to grind their grain

PIPING HOT Egyptian metal-workers, employed in jewellery-making, use blowpipes to boost the forge fire. Right: decorating a metal vessel.

RAG TRADE Women spin and weave at horizontal looms. Textile workshops existed from Old Kingdom times.

JEWELLERY WORK The craftsmen above are finishing a beaded collar or *wesekh.* Left: a gold bracelet from the tomb of Amosis. Right: a jewelled vulture adorns an 18th-dynasty pendant.

payments into flour. The men worked in shifts and their wages, chiefly paid in emmer wheat and barley, were boosted by supplements of fish, vegetables and water, and by wood for fuel and pottery for the home. A ration of grain came to about 475 lb (215 kg) a month, far more than the family needed, and the surplus was used in bartering for other goods. Extras included rations of cakes, beer and dates, while on festival days there were bonuses of salt, sesame oil and meat. The workmen had reasonable leisure time. Eight working days were followed by two days off when they rested, held parties and worked on their own tombs.

THE WORLD'S FIRST STRIKE

The men of Deir el-Medina often came into conflict with inefficient bureaucracy. Under the 20th Dynasty, they experienced many delays in the supply of their rations. When protests failed, the workforce withdrew its labour, downing tools in what has sometimes been called the world's first strike. This took place in Year 29 of the reign of Ramses III (*c.*1158 BC), and the most dramatic event was a strike in front of the royal

funerary temples. 'Hunger and thirst have driven us here,' the men complained angrily to the high priests. 'We have no clothing, oil, fish or vegetables. Write about it to our good lord the pharaoh, write about it to our master the vizier, and ask them to give us something to live on.'

During the unrest, a scribe called Amennakhte tried to reason with the men, and went himself to the Mortuary Temple of King Horemheb to get what

---

DID YOU KNOW?

The world's oldest map comes from ancient Egypt. It shows the gold mines of Wadi Hammamat in the south and dates back to the 20th dynasty (1186-1069 BC).

The Egyptians traded shipments of gold for a variety of foreign offerings. One pharaoh asked for 40 concubines 'in which there is no blemish and none with shrill voices'.

provisions he could for them. Should they accept the rather meagre supplies? There is evidence of divided loyalties among the foremen, for one of them suggested rather deviously that his men should take the provisions offered, but not get back to work. Mentmose, the chief of police, was supposed to encourage a return to work. Instead, he sided with the striking men, suggesting that they lock themselves behind closed doors with their wives and families. Some days later he even brought bread and beer for the strikers.

The papyrus describing the events is incomplete, so it is uncertain exactly how the affair ended. But it clearly challenges the stereotyped view of Egyptian working men as wholly downtrodden peasants struggling under an all-powerful ruler. Skilled workers, at least, knew the value of their labour.

Nonetheless, there certainly existed a class of labourers whose lot was unenviable by anybody's

TREASURE MAP Much of the gold that reached New Kingdom Egypt came from dry valleys to the south. The map shows the mines of Wadi Hammamat.

standards. Among these were the wretches who mined gold in the heat of the Nubian valleys. These people were captives – paupers, convicts and prisoners of war – who worked chained and naked along shafts gouged from the mountains. Guarded by soldiers and driven by the overseer's lash, they followed the gold-bearing quartz veins deep into the bowels of the rock. Whole families were involved: children carried back the hewn-out chippings; women and old men crushed the broken rock in mortars and grinders, and then washed the gold out on sloping tables or over stretched sheepskins. Our knowledge of their suffering comes chiefly from the reports of Diodorus the Sicilian, writing in the Graeco-Roman period of the 1st century BC. But it is easy to believe that conditions were much the same under the pharaohs.

BRINGING HOME THE BOOTY Men bearing tributes for the pharaoh from Nubia carry leopard skins and gold cast into rings.

KEEPING ORDER

The rule of law was respected in Egypt, and tough-minded policing helped to enforce it.

The ruling class lived in fear of social chaos when, in the words of one scribe,

'everyone shouts "I want" and the land perishes.'

AT ITS HEIGHT under the New Kingdom, the population of Egypt is reckoned to have numbered about 3 million. So large a figure called for a well-organised bureaucracy – and a substantial police force, too. A body of men known as the Medjay helped to keep order under the New Kingdom. They were, in origin, nomads from the Eastern Desert who had served as mercenaries in the Egyptian army; following campaigns against Asiatic invaders that ended in 1550 BC, the Medjay were regrouped as police units in Thebes and various other towns; the force was then enlarged under Ramses IV to cope with civil unrest, increasing raids by desert tribesmen – and a spate of tomb robberies.

If the Medjay were the enforcers, the law itself was the responsibility of the pharaoh. Theoretically, the god king was the fount of all legal decisions: in reality, though, he ruled through officials who drew for guidance on a body of precedents accumulated

MAN OF SUBSTANCE Ka-aper, a portly temple official, exudes shrewdness and authority in this wooden statue.

through the ages. In the reign of Thutmose III, legal decisions taken by a vizier about 500 years earlier were still remembered and enforced.

Everyday cases were brought before courts staffed by local worthies who heard complaints, witnessed contracts and arbitrated in disputes. They were not full-time lawyers – they might well spend the morning listening to court cases and the afternoon checking the state of the local reservoirs, scrutinising tax returns, and supervising the harvest of grain or the census of livestock. Nonetheless, the rule of law was honoured in Egyptian society, and even the common people often appealed to the courts to settle disputes.

Various types of legal papyrus have survived from the town of Kahun, covering a host of mundane matters: the *amt-pr* was a deed recording the transfer of property; the *aput* was an

HOLDING COURT Local officials arbitrated in everyday disputes, hearing cases in strict rotation.

HOW TO BE A SUCCESSFUL VIZIER

As the PHARAOH's right-hand men, the two viziers were Egypt's top officials. The job carried great responsibilities as well as privileges. The duties of the vizier are recorded in a set of tomb paintings:

❛ Look on your friend as a stranger and a stranger as your friend. The magistrate who acts like this will be successful. Do not pass over a petitioner, before you have considered his speech. When a petitioner is about to petition you, don't dismiss what he says as already said. If you refuse him, let him know why you refuse him. A man with a grievance likes his case to be heard sympathetically even more than he wants it put right. Do not scold a man wrongfully, scold where scolding is due. A real magistrate is always feared. But if people are positively frightened out of their wits by him, it can do his reputation a good deal of harm. People won't say of him: "There's a fine fellow!" You will be respected in your profession if you act strictly according to the dictates of justice. ❜

From the tomb of Rekhmire, vizier to Thutmose III

---

official register of a man's household, including family members, serfs and slaves; a third type was the *am remf* covering workmen and their superintendents, and recording, for example, the distribution of rations and the workmen's attendance at a given site; and the *sunu* was a fourth type, an official document appointing a government officer or engaging a servant.

Mild penalties were applied for minor offences against private property; for example, stolen or embezzled goods often had to be returned with a fine of twice their value. But the courts could be stern, too. Records from Deir el-Medina indicate that 100 or 200 strokes of the cane were a not unusual form of punishment, and that in serious cases five bleeding cuts, which would leave permanent scars, might be added, or ten brands inflicted as a lasting mark of shame. If an individual failed to turn up for communal work when summoned, he or she was often made to do forced labour permanently – or at least until a committee of review authorised release. If a runaway managed to evade capture, his or her family was carried off instead.

Cases were heard by the local courts in strict rotation, and serious crimes committed against temple or state would always be referred to a higher authority. In some cases, torture was used to extract a confession. Eight thieves who violated the tomb of King Sebekemsaf were cross-examined by being 'beaten with sticks both on their hands and feet' – an early example of the *bastinado*.

Other punishments included exile to Nubia or to some desert oasis, and mutilation – offenders might have their hands, tongue, nose or ears cut off. The death penalty was the ultimate sanction and, according to Diodorus, it could be applied in Egypt not only for the murder of a free man but also for that of a slave. Capital punishment took the form of decapitation, drowning, burning alive or impalement on the stake. The death penalty was not meted out lightly, however – it seems to have required the pharaoh's authorisation.

In sensitive cases, the pharaoh might bypass the orthodox legal channels and entrust a trial to a close confidant. It is clear that things happened in the royal

ROUGH JUSTICE A farmer is beaten for defaulting on taxes in this scene from an 18th-dynasty tomb of Menna.

WHEELING INTO BATTLE A fantasy scene shows the chariot-riding Tutankhamun driving Nubian enemies before him.

household that were best not put before the public. In the 6th dynasty, for example, a man named Weni, a favourite of King Pepy, recorded with considerable self-satisfaction:

'When there was a secret charge in the royal harem

against Queen Weret-yamtes, his majesty made me go in to hear it alone. No chief judge and no vizier, no official was there, only I alone; because I was worthy, because I was rooted in his majesty's heart; because his majesty had filled his heart with me. Only I put it in writing together with one other senior warden of Nekhen, while my rank was only that of an overseer of royal tenants. Never before had one like me heard a secret of the king's harem; but his majesty made me hear it, because I was worthy in his majesty's heart beyond any official of his, beyond any noble of his, beyond any servant of his.'

By the same token, it was sometimes thought more prudent to let an aristocratic offender commit suicide discreetly than have him face a public execution. The sentence passed on a figure in the harem conspiracy against Ramses III is terse and to the point:

'Pentawer, who formerly bore another name. He

ROUTE MARCH Infantrymen journey to Punt (probably on the Somali coast), where the Egyptians obtained gold, ivory and incense.

THE WAR CHARIOT

TWO-MAN WAR chariots with light, spoked wheels and a rear-set axle that permitted tight turning were introduced under the New Kingdom. The wickerwork body was open at the back, and the wheels were tyred with strips of leather. Many vehicles were splendidly decorated. It is clear that Egyptian nobles, who used their chariots for hunting and parades as well as in battle, took pride in their vehicles, for chariot-making is depicted in several New Kingdom tombs where carpenters, joiners and leather workers are all shown co-operating in the work.

In battle, the driver held the reins, whilst his partner fired arrows into the enemy to break their ranks. Massed infantry followed close behind, wielding hand weapons. Then, wheeling round for a second assault, the chariots charged in again to mop up enemy stragglers. It was a tactic the Egyptians borrowed from foreign armies, particularly that of Syria, and it seems to have been successful often enough. Ramses III boasted that his steeds 'quivered in all their limbs, prepared to crush the foreign countries under their hoofs'.

NOBLE CONVEYANCE
Aristocrats used chariots for parades and hunting, as well as battle.

was brought before the court, because he had joined with his mother Tey, when she conspired with the women of the harem, and because he acted with hostility against his lord. He was brought before the vassals, that they might question him. They found him guilty; they dismissed him to his house; he took his own life.'

EGYPT GOES TO WAR

Ultimately, the pharaoh's authority rested on his control of the armed forces. At times there were serious threats from desert peoples forced into the Nile valley by famine. A line of forts stretched along the western edge of the Delta to protect it from these migrations. To the south lay Nubia, a barren land through which the valuable luxuries of Sudan – ivory, ebony, incense and gold – passed northwards. At several periods the Egyptians occupied Nubia in order to control the transit of these goods. To this end, in about 2000 BC, the Egyptians built a series of massive fortresses in Nubia. But the powerful local kings always reasserted their control in the end, eventually conquering Egypt in about 710 BC and reigning as pharaohs themselves.

Large forts also guarded the frontiers of the eastern Delta, which was always vulnerable to attack by Asiatic invaders. Under the New Kingdom, pressure on this frontier caused the Egyptians to make pre-emptive strikes. They advanced as far as the River Euphrates, and conquered Syria and Palestine to meet the Hittite challenge. Egypt gradually acquired a sizable empire, hoards of imperial plunder – and a large, well-organised professional army.

At its height under Ramses II, the Egyptian army numbered about 20 000 men, organised in four divisions of 5000 men, each named after a god: Amun, Ptah, Seth and Re. The pharaoh was, of course, supreme commander, with a rigid chain of command beneath him: each division was composed of about 20 companies of 250 men, and each company in turn contained five platoons of 50 men. Spearsmen and archers made up the bulk of the troops, but the New Kingdom army also possessed horse-drawn chariots. The horse – first domesticated on the Ukrainian steppes – arrived in Egypt with a wave of Asiatic invaders called the Hyksos, who overran the Delta at the end of the Middle Kingdom. This nomadic people, known to the Egyptians as the Shepherd Kings, arrived via Palestine and Syria and had a big impact on society, bringing bronze technology as well as horsemanship.

Influenced by the new arrivals, the pharaohs started horse-breeding for themselves, and kings became very fond of their steeds, tending them personally in the royal stables (Ramses II had two favourites, named 'Theban Victory' and 'Mut is Content'). The Egyptians rarely, if ever, rode on horseback, however, using their horses mainly to draw chariots. The breeds of horse available at this time were small and light, and on the rare occasions that riders are shown in illustrations, they sit towards the rump, not in the middle of the back.

THE SOLDIER'S LIFE

Ownership of horses was for the elite. Most Egyptian troops were foot soldiers who traditionally fought bare-headed and seminaked behind cumbersome shields of wood covered with leather. Their spears, bows and copper axes were of low quality compared with the bronze scimitars and daggers, the body armour and powerful bows of the Hyksos. In fact, it was only by learning to handle the foreigners' equipment that the Egyptians were able to drive them out. Besides adopting bronze weapons, some Egyptian soldiers also acquired Asian-style helmets of bronze or leather as well as body armour, made from strips of leather stitched together in rows. When the Assyrians

---

A MAN OF COURAGE

King Seqenenre Tao, a 17th-dynasty pharaoh, gave his life in resisting the Hyksos invaders who overran the Delta. The skull fractures on his mummy exactly match the cross-section of the type of battle axe used by the Hyksos, and a spear thrust behind his left ear probably dispatched him. Forensic study has revealed a man of considerable courage. The bone around one gash at the top of his forehead had already begun to heal before the time of death, and an arm was already contorted from the brain damage. Evidently, the pharaoh had been badly wounded in an earlier encounter – yet he went forth to fight nonetheless.

AN EGYPTIAN FOOT SOLDIER ON CAMPAIGN

THEY BEGAN THE MARCH at dawn. Wakened by the blare of a trumpet, Paser quickly put on his mail coat of wadded leather, and a thick leather cap for a helmet. He gathered up his lance and sickle-shaped sword, lugged his heavy shield from the ground and slung it over his back.

Paser was a native Egyptian from a peasant family in the farmlands that adjoined the marshes of the Delta. He had been called to arms by a royal recruiting officer who came one day to his village, pressing one man in ten into compulsory service. Resistance was futile – a youth who had attempted it was clubbed senseless by two dark-skinned Nubians who came with the recruiting unit.

Life at the training barracks was an ordeal of which Paser could remember little but the beatings, the boredom, and the misery of being marched in step endlessly back and forth under the eye of a bullying drill-master. After that, active service had come almost as a relief. Paser had fought against Syrians and against the marauding tribesmen of the Eastern Desert. Often he had done garrison service at the frontier fortress of Tjel, sometimes escorting expeditions to the copper mines of Sinai. Now they were marching through Sinai again, this time against the Hittites.

At midday the troops rested. Paser ate a frugal lunch of barley bread and water, eked out with some onions and curds. A reported sighting of enemy troops caused some alarm among the younger men in his unit, but Paser was not alarmed as rumours were part of life on the march. When they continued in the afternoon, he saw the full strength of the columns stretching before and behind: the units of spearsmen, the archers, the axemen, the supply service, the foreign auxiliaries and the charioteers with their gleaming vehicles and tasselled steeds. Paser had come to take pride in some aspects of soldiering. Although he had finished his term of compulsory service, he did not think he could return to the monotony of peasant life – not at least without the grant of land he hoped to get as a pension.

They covered over 20 miles (32 km) that day, and by the time dusk began to settle on the rugged landscape, every throat was parched with thirst. But the sight of several straggly palms and acacia trees on the horizon signalled the well where they were to camp that night. Before darkness fell, the troops had gathered their rations of water from the desert spring, pitched their tents and lit their fires.

The younger men fell asleep after eating and Paser longed for slumber too, but he had been posted for sentry duty. The desert air suddenly grew cold. He wrapped a coarse linen blanket around him and scanned the moonlit terrain. His day was not over yet.

SPEARMEN
The army depended on auxiliaries like these, depicted in a tomb model.

and Persians launched fierce onslaughts with their hard, iron weapons, the bronze-bearing Egyptians were again caught unprepared. The Iron Age was late in coming to Egypt, as iron was not naturally available there.

Many of Egypt's soldiers were young conscripts levied against their will. On arrival at the barracks they would have their hair cut to a regulation helmet-like shape and embark on a tough preparation course. Recruits did training in physical exercise, wrestling and the use of weapons. They also endured severe beatings for breaches of discipline, and it is hardly surprising that some of the peasant boys called up for military service absconded at the first opportunity. Nonetheless, there were keen volunteers, too, for whom the army represented secure employment and the hope of advancement.

Rewards were made both to officers and men who had shown valour in the field – not just medals, but pensions, promotion, grants of land and awards of slaves were among the forms of payment that seasoned campaigners might expect to receive on retirement. In fact, a military career was so appealing to some that the scribes felt it necessary to describe its abominations, in order to dissuade their own pupils from rejecting more peaceable professions and taking up arms instead:

REGISTERING DISAPPROVAL **The scribes evidently regarded the army as a threat to their own authority.**

Come, let me tell you how the soldier fares

with his many superiors – the general, the commander of the auxiliaries, the standard-bearer, the lieutenant, the captains of 50, and the commander of the garrison troops. Come let me tell you how he marches over the mountains to Palestine. His bread and water are carried on his back like the load of an ass. His drink consists of foul water. He falls out only for picket duty. When he reaches the enemy he is like a pinioned bird and has no strength in his limbs. If he returns to Egypt he is like worm-eaten wood. He is

brought back on an ass: his kit has been stolen and his servant has run off.

As for the noble charioteer:

He squanders his patrimony on an expensive chariot that he drives furiously. When he has acquired a fine span of horses he is overjoyed and tears madly around his home town with them. When he reaches the mountains he has to cast his expensive chariot into the thicket and go on foot. When he reports back he is beaten with a hundred blows.

The nation's new military ambitions certainly brought about changes. For the first time in Egyptian history a number of pharaohs spent a lot of their time campaigning outside their own country. Additionally, more and more foreigners were drawn into the Egyptian armies. Some were mercenaries, others foreign captives who could win their eventual freedom through a period of military service. Kushites from Nubia and Sudan, Libyans, people from western Asia – the Sheklesh and Sherdern (who probably later colonised Sardinia) – and, much later, Greeks all saw service under the pharaoh.

Egypt in the New Kingdom became more cosmopolitan than ever before – and it became much richer too. The soldier-pharaohs gave gigantic donations of war plunder to the priesthood, and it was during this era that colossal temples were built at Thebes. Around 1550 BC Thebes became the most important city of southern Egypt, and one of the three 'capital' cities, the others being Heliopolis (near modern Cairo) and Memphis. Much of the wealth of the Egyptian Empire flowed into the treasuries of its temples, and the kings were buried in a secret valley in the mountains on the opposite bank of the Nile to Thebes. The city of Amun, whose vast temple was filled with colossal statues and towering obelisks plated with gold, was famous throughout the ancient world – to Homer it was 'Hundred-gated Thebes' and to the Biblical prophets 'No-Ammon'.

EGYPTIAN COUNTRY LIFE

Two field workers pack harvested corn into rope baskets, all ready to be
carried back to the threshing building. The great achievements of the
pharaohs would have been impossible without men like these, burned black
through toiling under the sun in the vast quilt of fields bordering the Nile.
Agriculture was Egypt's primary source of wealth – numberless baskets
of wheat and barley were at the basis of her civilisation.

THE FARMING CALENDAR

Hardly a drop of rain fell on the pharaohs' land. Only the annual cataclysm

of the flood – and the patient, year-round work of irrigation by the farmers –

allowed crops to flourish under the desert sky.

THE RHYTHMS of village life in ancient Egypt barely changed over the millennia. Whatever the hardships, there was a continuity in the braying of the donkeys outside the mud-brick huts; the routine chores of baking the bread and making the beer; the sound of the village potters slapping and pounding the Nile clay; and the sight of the fishermen casting their nets into the river. Egyptian civilisation may have been shaped in the handful of bustling towns. But the country remained essentially agricultural, and the great mass of the people were field workers eking out a simple existence in partnership with their livestock. Day after day they followed their quiet rounds of toil in the dust and sun with little to disturb their lives except seasonal change – in particular, the drama of the deluge.

In the Season of Flood the pharaohs' realm became a drowned land. Vast tracts of farming country simply vanished under water, leaving villages standing out as islands in an immense river-fed lake. The inundation began at the onset of summer (about June 19 of the modern calendar) and was signalled in the heavens by the reappearance on the horizon of the 'Dog Star', Sirius, which had been out of sight for weeks. Thereafter – all being well – the Nile waters

FLOOD WARNING

Shortly before the flood season began in Egypt, flocks of white ibises appeared, returning from their southerly migration. The Egyptians interpreted this as a sign of divine knowledge on the birds' part – which was perhaps why the wise god Thoth was given the head of an ibis.

would rise steadily, reaching their height around mid-August. This was the time for farmers to row around their dykes, shutting the vents to pen the waters and their deposits of mud. The flood season was the time for major building works. As no one could work on the land, the men were taken to cut stone and ship it to the temple sites; during this period, they and their families were fed from the state stores.

There were three seasons in Egypt's farming year, each lasting four months. After the flood came the seasons of Going Out and of Harvest. Ploughing and sowing were done in the Season of Going Out, when the flood subsided and farmers opened the vents in their dykes to let out the last of the water. As soon as the ground was firm enough to walk on, the villagers started turning it to prepare for the sowing of seed. Timing was important, for if the mud was left too long, the desert sun would bake it as hard as rock. So they began in the fields with the last pools of water

TURNING THE EARTH   The plough, introduced into Egypt around 2500 BC, was hand-operated as well as being drawn by cattle.

FLOOD SEASON At the time of the annual deluge, much of Egypt vanished under water.

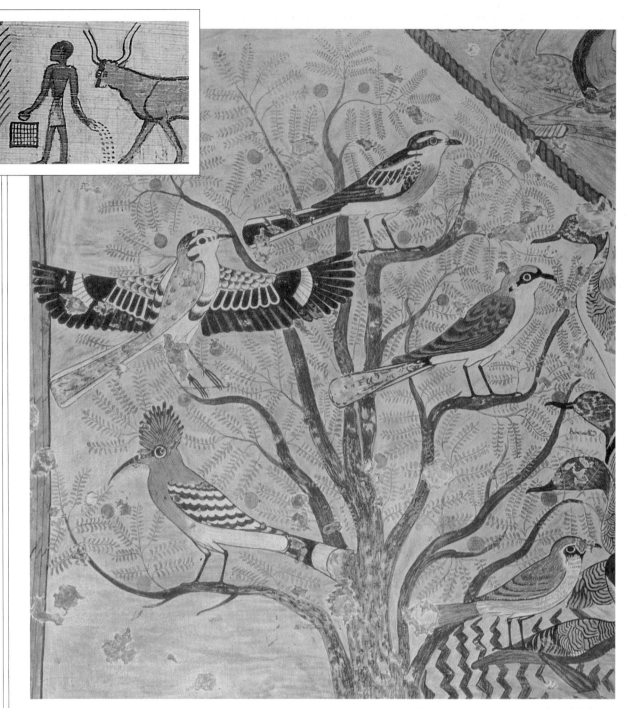

BIRD LIFE Egypt teemed with bird species. Inset: cattle trample seed into the fields, partly to protect it from birds.

still glimmering on the ground, using hoes or light wooden ploughs to make the moist soil ready.

The plough itself consisted of a hard wooden blade fixed to a pair of wooden poles splayed outwards at the top, with a long shaft connecting them to the yoke. The ploughman guided the plough from behind, pressing down on it with all his might with one hand and wielding a whip in the other to urge his team on. Cattle were used as draught animals.

A 19th-dynasty tomb scene shows ploughmen chatting to each other as they go about their business. 'What a beautiful, mild day! The team is pulling well. The gods are helping us. Let us work hard for our master.' The cheery tone in this and other tomb paintings probably reflects the artist's desire to please their noble patrons. In reality, field work must have been hard and, labouring half-naked in the pitiless sun, the villagers were exposed to a multitude of ailments. While wading about in the muddy waters of pools and canals, for example, they fell prey to

PAPYRUS – THE PLANT OF HAPPINESS

DENSE THICKETS of papyrus lined the banks of the Nile and the broad marshes of the Delta. The tall, reed-like plant, grew well over head height and was an all-purpose provider in ancient Egypt, used to make numerous everyday items such as baskets, mats, sieves and sandals. Long stems of papyrus were bound together in bundles to make boats, and their fibres were beaten flat to make sails or twisted into cordage for rigging. People even cooked and ate the pith of the plant, while they burned the root for fuel.

Culturally, the most fruitful use of papyrus was in fashioning paper, which the Egyptians learnt to make as early as 3500 BC. First, the rind was stripped from the stalk of the reed, and the pith sliced lengthwise into strips. After soaking, these were laid side by side in one layer, then another layer of strips was placed on top of them at right angles. A covering cloth was then placed over the sheet and the papyrus was pounded with a wooden mallet, the starch in the plant's juices forming a natural adhesive. A number of sheets pasted end to end formed a long roll.

Lightweight and easy to handle, papyrus rolls were far more adaptable than the baked clay tablets used for writing in Mesopotamia. The Egyptians monopolised the production of this valuable commodity, and exported it in bulk. The word paper stems from the Greek *papuros*.

The Egyptians were well aware of the debt they owed this bountiful plant, and expressed their gratitude in many ways. Papyrus was so widespread in the Delta that it became the symbolic plant of Lower Egypt (the sedge was the emblem of Upper Egypt). When the stalk had been used for one or other of its multifarious purposes, the head furnished garlands for the shrines of the gods. In mythology the papyrus represented the earth arising from the primeval ocean. People also wore amulets in the shape of bundled papyrus for magical protection – it was a guarantee of youth and happiness.

PAPERWORK Strips of papyrus are pounded to make paper – one of Egypt's most important exports.

parasitic bilharzia worms, whose larvae burrow through the skin to enter the blood system with debilitating results. Snakes and scorpions were a menace in the fields, and spells against them were a major feature of Egyptian magic.

SCATTERING THE SEED

Before sowing could start, a scribe in charge of the granaries carefully recorded the rations of grain apportioned to each farmer, for purposes of taxation. Then, at the order of the village headman, the sowing ceremony began. This was a ritual symbolising the burial of Osiris, the murdered god whose body had been cut into pieces and scattered throughout the length and breadth of Egypt. Osiris was later brought back to life by his wife and sister, the goddess Isis, and to Egyptians, the burial of grain and its sprouting afresh recalled the god's death and resurrection.

When all the rites had been properly observed, the farmers then cast the seed over the broken earth. Afterwards, herdsmen drove their pigs, sheep or goats over the fields to tread the seed in with their hooves. Then came the long and arduous task of keeping the growing crops watered. In the Old and Middle Kingdom periods, buckets were carried to the fields from dawn to dusk – a tedious chore. In the New

levels could have a profound impact on Egyptian society. For example, it has been suggested that low waters at the start of the First Intermediate Period so wrecked the economy that it took nearly 200 years to recover prosperity during the Middle Kingdom. Egyptian life was quickened again by high floods that unblocked silted-up water courses, causing the Nile's waters to reach fields that had long been out of action.

Overflooding could be equally damaging, breaching dykes and sweeping away mud-brick houses, ruining seed stores and even surging into the stone-built temples. The swollen waters caused a delay in sowing, so that crops might later be scorched by the midsummer sun. And the resulting dampness increased the risk of insect plagues, which could destroy a crop. Even after a good flood season, a year's work could be ruined by a flash storm that flattened the grain as it ripened. An exceptional flood in 684 BC came without the usual problems: 'Amun-Re has given me good cultivation throughout, he has destroyed the vermin and the snakes within it, he has kept away locusts, and he has not allowed the south winds to reap it. I have reaped for the Double Granary an incalculable harvest of Upper Egyptian and Lower Egyptian barley.'

HARVEST TIME

In a good year, the crops grew tall and ripened in fields of gold. The bounty of the Nile was collected in the Season of Harvest, when the people of every village – men, women and children – left home by

Kingdom, the monotony was lessened by the introduction of a pole and bucket device, the *shaduf*.

In a bad year the floods might fail, leaving the thirsty fields starved of their rich mud deposits. Recent studies have shown that a decline in flood

THE FIRST CUT **The pharaoh reaped the first stalks of corn to mark the onset of the harvest.**

WINNOWING An 18th-dynasty scene shows corn being tossed to separate the chaff from the grain.

the chaff. The last stage was winnowing, in which the trampled ears were shovelled up in wooden scoops and tossed into the air so that the wind carried off the last of the chaff while the clean grain fell to earth.

A celebrated painting from the Theban tomb of Menna, a Scribe of the Fields, shows the harvest being carried out under his supervision. Dating from the 15th century BC, the picture includes humorous glimpses of a boy snoozing under a tree, and two girls quarrelling over pieces of wheat that the reapers have left behind, tugging at one another's hair in their vexation. Menna himself watches from under a shady canopy, while a servant brings him a flask of cool drink. A tranquil scene, perhaps, but the scribe was not a wholly benevolent presence at the harvest. Once the crop had been gathered and winnowed, the official would bring out standard wooden tubs to measure the quantities of grain. If a farmer could not – or would not – give up the quantity required as tax, he was likely to be

dawn light and went out to gather in the ready corn. Foreign captives and even army units were also drafted in at times, with the state taking a keen interest in all that went on. Before work could begin, tax assessors came to gauge the expected yield and fix the quantities to be taken as dues. It was important to calculate the likely as well as the actual yield, for parts of the harvest might easily 'go astray'.

Harvest began with rites honouring Min, the Egyptian god of masculine fertility, who was represented with an erect phallus and wielding a flail. During the official state ceremony, the pharaoh himself took up a sickle to reap the first ears of grain. Then the harvesters would advance into the standing corn, the men wielding the sickles to cut off the ears at the top of the stalk. The women followed, gathering the handfuls of corn in baskets, while the children gleaned at their feet. All moved steadily forward to the rhythm of a harvest song, sung by one of the team while the other harvesters chanted the response; sometimes a flute player provided an accompaniment.

The sheaves of corn were then loaded into nets or baskets and carried on donkeyback to the threshing floor. This was a circle of stamped earth, enclosed by a low wall, where the corn was forked out to be trampled by cattle in order to loosen the grain from

TEETH OF THE HARVEST

Some Egyptian sickles consisted of real animals' jawbones, with flints set in the tooth sockets. Others were made of suitably shaped wood, grooved so that a line of flint 'teeth' could be inserted. One such sickle, found at the pyramid-workmen's town of Kahun, was custom-made for a left-handed reaper.

THE RECKONING Scribes on a nobleman's estate calculate the size of the harvest for tax purposes.

SHIPS THAT PLIED THE NILE

THE NILE was Egypt's main highway. Wherever people wanted to go – to travel from the country to town, to visit temple or palace, or to travel between cities – there was only really one route for a journey of any distance. No roads of any size are known to have existed; and there were no bridges over the main stream – just ferries plying incessantly back and forth across the river. The wheel was certainly known in ancient Egypt, and was in later times skilfully adapted for war chariots. But for purposes of transport, the Egyptians scarcely bothered with it. Communication over any distance meant the Nile.

The boats that went up and down the busy highway were aided by two convenient natural energy resources: the wind and the river current. Egypt's prevailing wind blew from north to south, so that ships heading upstream travelled with their sails up. Coming downstream, mast and sail were removed, and the ship was carried northwards by the current, aided by rows of oarsmen. This was such a fixed pattern of travel that in Egyptian writing, the hieroglyph of a ship in full sail meant 'going south' and that of a ship with no sail meant 'going north'.

The different types of ship had certain general features in common. The broad rectangular sail was operated by the crew or by a man at the stern, who tugged at a lanyard to catch the breeze; the large steering oar was also operated from the stern. At the prow stood the pilot, holding a long pole with which he sounded the depth of the water. Rowers seated along the gunwales propelled the boat when the ship was travelling downstream.

The first boats were made of reeds or papyrus, and vessels of these materials remained in use for getting about in shallow, marshy waters. Wood was scarce in Egypt, though local acacia could be sawn into planks to build the sturdy little ships that were common carriers for the farmers' wine and corn. At the other end of the scale, huge rafts were needed by the priests for transporting statues of the gods from one temple to another, and to float stone for pyramids and obelisks along the Nile. For bigger vessels, cedars of Lebanon were floated down from Byblos, the port in the Near East with which they did most business. These great trees yielded large, thick planks that allowed boatmakers to create such magnificent vessels as the funeral barge of Khufu, the 4th-dynasty pharaoh who built the Great Pyramid at Giza.

Unlike the ancient peoples of, for example, Crete and Phoenicia, the Egyptians were not keen seafarers. Nonetheless, they did build some maritime vessels, equipped with extra strengthening timbers to withstand the pounding of the waves. They also made warships for army use, capable of carrying up to 250 men. Officers had their own cabins, and the oarsmen were protected by parapets running along the decks, rowing through gaps in the timbers. In an engagement fought near the mouth of the Nile in 1174 BC, Ramses III repelled an armada of Mediterranean seafarers, the pharaoh setting up a wall of defence with warships, galleys and skiffs packed with infantrymen. A relief shows them raining arrows on the invading swordsmen and spearsmen, some of whom are hit and fall headlong into the water.

FULL SAIL A funeral vessel carries the mummy of Sennefer, mayor of Thebes, along the Nile to Abydos for burial according to the proper rites.

QUIET MOMENT **A worker dozes under a tree while a companion plays a flute. Right: raking out the harvested wheat.**

cruelly beaten. One such defaulter is shown being thrashed in the painting from Menna's tomb, and the scene is not unique.

Such punishment seems to have been fairly routine. An Egyptian text describes how 'the scribe-officer arrives to count up the harvest; he has bailiffs with him who wield sticks, and black men with palm stalks. "Give us the grain," they say. "There is none." So they hold him by the legs and beat him, then tie him up and throw him in the ditch. His wife is bound too, and his children, and their neighbours make haste to abandon them so as to save their own grain.' An oppressive tax collector was the bane of country life, but there must have been cases in which farmers were justly accused of withholding what they owed to the state. And the officials' ruthlessness can also be explained in part by the fact that the farmers

did not own the fields that they worked. All the land in Egypt belonged to the pharaoh, or to the temple authorities and nobles to whom he granted it. The scribes knew that harshness might be counter-productive. A New Kingdom text known as the *Loyalist Teaching* advises: 'Do not make the labourer wretched with taxes; enrich him and he will be there for you the next year. If he lives you are in his hands. If you bring him low he will become a fugitive.'

Once the harvest was complete, the greater part of the grain was taken off in sacks and poured into state or temple granaries. These were the powerhouses of ancient Egypt's economy, whose stocks of surplus grain fed the multitudes not engaged in field work: soldiers, priests, palace staff, building workers and

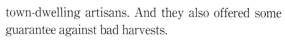

town-dwelling artisans. And they also offered some guarantee against bad harvests.

Between the main grain harvest in March or April and the onset of the next floods, farmers had time to grow a second crop – often of the pulses and vegetables that varied their diet. In addition to wheat and barley, flax was a third staple, providing the linen which clothed the Egyptians. Flax was pulled from the ground rather than cut, and harvested at different times according to its future use. Young plants were best for making fine thread, while the mature crop was better suited to coarse fabrics, ropes and matting.

AT THE GRANARY **An 11th-dynasty limestone carving shows officials carefully recording the amount of corn being brought by the porters to the grain store.**

FROM DELTA TO DESERT

Cattle grazed in the lush meadows of the Delta, while sheep nibbled the leaner

pasturelands at the desert edge. Drovers and shepherds, fishermen and fowlers,

all were familiar figures in Egyptian country life.

THE LORD AND HIS FAMILY lived in a square-built villa that was more than just a private dwelling; with its teeming servants' quarters, workshops, kitchens, stables and shrines, it resembled, rather, a little township. No country villas have been excavated, but the officials' houses at Amana probably followed the same plan. There the whole compound was normally walled, with a single entrance and stout wooden doors which had to be opened for visitors by estate workers at the caretaker's lodge. Inside, servants were always busy with a variety of tasks, herding the geese, taking grain to the beehive-shaped silos, tidying the guest rooms and repairing the ploughs. The estate was a self-contained world with carpenters to make any necessary furniture, gardeners to tend the palm-edged vegetable beds – and scribes, of course, to check the quantities of everything that was grown, made, bartered or stored there. The entire establishment was managed by the lord's steward, and a vintner, too, was often employed to oversee the production of the lord's wine. Grapes might be grown in separate

FORDING A STREAM One herdsman carries a bleating calf ahead, to entice the others across. The second herdsman wears a lifejacket of bundled reeds.

vineyards, or in the garden, where vines might be twined around poles, trained over pergolas or set against the walls.

The whitewashed villa at the centre of the compound might have as many as 30 rooms including the great hall, stores, bedrooms and harem. The workrooms, servants' huts and stables were grouped some distance away, with the cow pens close by. Beyond the walls lay the cornfields and pasturelands to which the cattle were led. Stockbreeding was a

CATTLE COUNT A tomb model shows the census of cattle on a great estate. Officials watch from a dais as the herd is marched past.

COUNTRY HOUSE Rural villas like this were self-supporting, with their own food supplies and workshops.

widespread occupation, and the drovers and shepherds seem to have lived particularly comfortless lives. Those depicted in tomb scenes sometimes appear balding and unshaven – an unusual break with the artistic convention by which a nobleman's estate workers usually appeared neat and healthy. Being constantly on the move with their herds, they must have seemed to ordinary farmers a rootless, dishevelled class. They can often be identified in paintings by their tucked-up kilts, and by the staff they are carrying over their shoulders, from which hangs a roll of matting to provide protection against the elements.

The longer migrations in search of pasture

EGYPTIAN RAM This image from the *Book of the Dead* depicts the long-legged breed of sheep native to Egypt.

involved the crossing and recrossing of river and canals, often terminating at the fine grazing land found on the broad expanses of the Nile Delta. Both long-horned and short-horned cattle were bred by the Egyptians and, during the New Kingdom, the hump-backed Brahman bull arrived from western Asia, introduced perhaps to improve breeding stock. Cattle had to be penned or guarded at night to protect them from thieves and predators, and while grazing during the day they were tethered by ropes of twisted date-palm fibre to stones buried in the ground. A bull or cow was a prized possession, being the most valuable animal on an estate, and no risks could be taken with one: from the 18th Dynasty, farmers had their cattle branded, using bronze branding irons, as marks of ownership.

The cattle count was a key event in every estate's calendar, and in the Old Kingdom it was even used to number the years of a king's reign, Year One being the 'year of the first cattle count'. In the Middle Kingdom, wooden tomb models of estates often showed the census. One example comes from the 11th-dynasty tomb of Meketre, a wealthy Theban nobleman. The lord is seated on a dais with the chief herdsman bowing before him, while four scribes record the numbers of cattle as they are marched past in single file. In yet another tomb painting, a herdsman who is bringing cattle

before the scribe is told by a companion not to waste time arguing with the official, for 'he is a fair man and will assess you properly. He is not hard on folk.'

SACRED BULL AND RAM-HEADED GOD

The temples reared huge herds of cattle for ritual use in sacrifice, and the creatures had important religious associations. The goddess Hathor was represented as a cow, sometimes suckling a royal infant at her udder. And during the Late Period at Memphis, a bull called Apis became the focus of a major animal cult; the black bull, which had a white triangle on its forehead and other distinctive marks on its tongue and flank, was regarded as an earthly manifestation of the creator god Ptah. Priests tended each Apis with infinite care, and from time to time the creature would be let out so that its behaviour could be studied for signs and omens.

Pampered during its lifetime, the Apis was mummified at death and transported with great ceremony to Saqqara. Here it was laid to rest in an underground tomb called the Serapeum, specially created for the interment of sacred bulls. The priests conducted rites to free the bull's *ka*, or spirit, and afterwards initiated a search for the animal's successor – a bull with similar markings. The cult continued until the 2nd century AD and, though the Serapeum was subsequently buried in the sands, it was to be rediscovered in 1851 by the French Egyptologist Auguste Mariette. When its network of vaults and galleries were reopened, Mariette came upon colossal granite sarcophagi,

APIS BULL The bronze figure represents a bull, regarded as the living emblem of the god Ptah.

HOW TO CATCH A CROCODILE SAFELY

❝Of the numerous different ways of catching crocodiles I will describe the one which seems to me the most interesting. They bait a hook with a chine of pork and let it float out into midstream, and at the same time, standing on the bank, beat a live pig to make it squeal. The crocodile makes a rush towards the squealing pig, encounters the bait, gulps it down, and is hauled out of the water. The first thing the huntsman does when he has got the beast on land is to plaster its eyes with mud; this done, it is dispatched easily enough – but without this precaution it will give a lot of trouble. ❞

SOBEK The crocodile god, shown in a statuette from the Ptolemaic period.

From *The Histories* by Herodotus

---

some weighing 6 tons, in which the mummified remains of 64 Apis bulls had been buried.

Sheep and goats were familiar features of the rural scene, flourishing on leaner pasturelands than those favoured by cattle. The native sheep was herded in Egypt from prehistory. Rather tall, with long, spiral horns that extended horizontally from the head, it came to be seen as an incarnation of the ram-headed god Khnum, who had fashioned mankind upon the potter's wheel and whose main temple stood on the island of Elephantine near Egypt's southern frontier. By New Kingdom times, the native sheep had been replaced by an imported variety that was lower-built, with curly horns set close to the head. The farm pig (evolved from the wild boar) was rarely represented in Egyptian paintings, yet pig-herding was obviously widespread.

WILDLIFE OF DESERT AND MARSH

The Egyptians lived much closer to nature than modern Westerners do, and the distinction between wild and domesticated animals was more blurred. Besides the cattle, sheep, goats and geese raised on the farm, experiments were made in domesticating

TENT-DWELLERS Herdsmen kept on the move, following their animals on long migrations in search of pasture.

TOMB GUARDIAN Jackal-headed Anubis, god of the dead, weighs the heart or soul of a deceased man against the feather of truth.

animals such as antelope, oryx and hyena – creatures from the wilderness beyond the cornfields.

Westwards lay the Libyan desert, a vast eroded tableland notched by a line of fertile depressions containing oases fed from the Nile's water table. Eastwards loomed the barren mountains of the Arabian desert gouged by deep *wadis*, or dry watercourses. Winter storms occasionally caused them to run as torrents, so that water spilled out and the stony ground suddenly became carpeted with desert flowers. Otherwise, the vegetation was scorched almost to extinction, the sparse, dry grasses supporting only the wandering Bedouin and their flocks.

The desert extended over thousands of square miles, and its lonely, forbidding immensities of rock and sand caused the settled farming folk to shudder. Untouched by the

DESERT CHASE A dog runs after a hyena in this sketch done on limestone.

annual miracle of the flood, the baleful landscape reached the very edge of the fields, and it was to this disquieting zone that the dead were taken for burial. The desert always remained a place of death in the Egyptian mind. Jackals haunted the wilderness, finding their way into popular belief in the shape of Anubis – the jackal-headed guardian of tombs. No doubt his role as a god of the dead derived from the fact that the jackal dug up human bones. In early times, the Egyptians piled stones on the graves of their loved ones to keep them safe from the jackals'

attentions. By making a jackal god guardian of their dead, the Egyptians sought to propitiate the creature most likely to disturb them.

Egypt's marshlands represented a completely contrasting landscape. The flat, low-lying plain of the Delta, crosshatched by the many branches of the Nile, fanned out over some 200 miles (320km). Lush as its pastures were, much of the land was too waterlogged to be cultivated, and dense, mosquito-plagued reedbeds sprawled to the horizon. The marshes teemed with life: frogs, eels, fishes, mongooses, chameleons, wildcats and waterbirds moved among the drifts of lotus and thickets of papyrus.

Egyptian fishermen went angling in papyrus canoes, using rods and lines fitted with hooks of bone or bronze. They set out traps, too, made of plaited reed stems, or trawled the river with weighted drag nets. Fowlers also used nets to catch water birds, sometimes baiting the ground with corn, sometimes casting a net over a pool. A colourful variety of wildfowl frequented the marshes – wild ducks, geese, plovers, snipe, herons, cranes – and all were fair game. The fowlers were particularly skilled in the use of the clapnet – a net with a drawstring and a sprung wooden frame which could be pulled shut over the catch. One of the men would hide by the appointed spot and wave a cloth to tell his companions when to pull the drawstring.

Crocodiles lurked in the marshlands and river alike. The Greek historian Herodotus wrote a long and fascinating account of this scaly, outlandish reptile with 'eyes like a pig's and great fang-like teeth'. He also noted an interesting detail well known to modern zoologists:

One result of its spending so much time in the water is that the inside of its mouth gets covered with leeches. Other animals avoid the crocodile, as do all birds too with one exception – the sandpiper, or Egyptian plover: this bird is of service to the crocodile and lives, in consequence, in the greatest amity with him;

PERILS IN THE FIELDS

ROMAN HISTORIANS record that the beautiful Egyptian Queen Cleopatra took her own life by applying an asp to her bosom. This seems to have been a traditional means that people in Egypt used to commit suicide, though the serpent mentioned in the histories is less likely to have been an asp (native to southern Europe) than an Egyptian cobra.

Snakes were among the most worrying of all the perils of daily life in ancient Egypt. And of all snakes the most dreaded was undoubtedly *Naja haje* – the Egyptian cobra – with its sinister hood, which it formed by expanding the skin of its neck. Spasms, paralysis and death resulted from the cobra's bite, and people were so afraid of it that the creature came to symbolise another awesome fact of Egyptian life: the pharaoh's power over his subjects. The cobra was represented in the Uraeus – the figure of the sacred serpent that was depicted in the pharaoh's headdress, coiled at his brow and ready to spit its fiery venom at any opponent.

In Egypt, as in a number of other early societies, the danger posed by a lethal creature was confronted by turning it into a god. Because a

SACRED EMBLEM A cobra badge in gold and lapis lazuli comes from the headdress of the pharaoh Sesostris II.

snake could be worshipped, it could also be propitiated – and when necessary could even be turned against the worshipper's enemies. So, villagers who lived in dread of the cobras that they often found in the ripe corn came to worship Renenutet, a snake goddess of fertility who presided over the harvest. She was depicted as a cobra, or a cobra-headed woman. To give thanks for a successful harvest, estate owners were required to make offerings to her in the form of corn, birds, bread, cucumbers, melons and other gifts.

Sand vipers and horned vipers also threatened the villagers of the Nile valley. In fact, a list of serpents drawn up during the Late Period catalogues just about every Egyptian species of snake known to modern science, complete with a detailed account of the appearance and particular dangers of each. The Egyptians were very fearful of snakes, and even thought that they existed in the afterlife – spells were made to repel them in the realm of the dead:

> *Get back! Crawl away! Get away from me, you snake! Go,*

SNAKES ALIVE A fear of serpents haunted Egyptians, who dreaded meeting them, even in the afterlife.

be drowned in the Lake of the Abyss, at the place where your father commanded that the slaying of you should be carried out. Be far removed from that abode of Re wherein you trembled, for I am Re at whom men tremble; get back, you rebel, at the knives of light . . . Fall! Crawl away, Apep, you enemy of Re! O you who escape massacre in the east of the sky at the sound of the roaring storm . . . Get back! You shall be decapitated with a knife, your face shall be cut away all round, your head shall be removed by him who is in his land, your bones shall be broken . . .

The risks for field workers did not end with snakes. Scorpions lurked under stones, their tails tipped with a venomous sting, and they, too, were duly incorporated into folklore and religion. In one myth the goddess Isis travels about the countryside with an escort of seven scorpions; when a wealthy woman refuses the goddess shelter, the scorpions sting her infant son. However, Isis, the divine mother, cannot contemplate the death of an innocent child and recites a healing spell that names the scorpions one by one: Petet, Tjetet, Matet, Mesetet, Mesetetef, Tefen and Befen. Through the process of naming the scorpions, the goddess gains dominance over them. The words of her spell were recited to anyone who had a child suffering from a scorpion sting, while a medical preparation of barley bread, garlic and salt was applied.

DUCKS AND GEESE Wildfowl burst from thickets of papyrus in a wall painting from the royal palace at Amarna. Right: a bean goose grazes in the meadows.

for when the crocodile comes ashore and lies with his mouth wide open (which he generally does facing towards the west), the bird hops in and swallows the leeches. The crocodile enjoys this, and never, in consequence, hurts the bird.

Humans enjoyed no such friendly relationship. Crocodiles were an ever-present threat to anyone whose work took him or her to the waterside – as the *Satire on Trades* makes clear, describing the creatures as a threat to laundry workers, and to Nile fishermen who might suddenly succumb to the terrible jaws 'as if struck by the hand of God'. The crocodile loomed large in the national psyche, and the Egyptians worshipped a crocodile god, Sobek, as a deity of water and vegetation. The cult was widespread from the Delta to the First Cataract, but its special centre was a city called Crocodilopolis (Shedet) in the Faiyum. Here, in the temple pool, a living crocodile was kept as a representative of the deity, adorned with gold rings and fed on ceremonial offerings.

Another spectacular denizen of river and marsh was the hippopotamus. Herodotus marvelled at the ox-like immensity of this animal with a hide so thick and tough 'that when dried it can be made into spear-shafts'. Perhaps it was the pugnacity of the mother that caused them to worship the hippopotamus godess, Taweret, as the protector of women in childbirth. For the ancient Egyptians, the restless giant of the Nile seemed to embody all the power of wild, unpredictable nature.

HIPPOPOTAMUS The huge mammal, depicted in a faience sculpture, was feared and respected by the Egyptians.

THE EGYPTIANS AT PLAY

'Make holiday!' was the cry in the ancient Egyptian Harper's Song. The people of the Nile knew how to enjoy themselves, as this 18th-dynasty tomb painting from West Thebes amply demonstrates. Whether enjoying a lavish feast, swaying to music, roistering at festival time, watching boxing or wrestling matches, listening to the fantastic tales of storytellers or hunting hippopotamus in the marshes, the Egyptians threw themselves with relish into their leisure pursuits.

BANQUETS, BOOKS AND GAMES

For all the fragrant perfumes and the elegant furniture, a feast was often a

disorderly event at which guests ate and drank themselves sick. Many must have turned with relief to

the quieter delights of books and board games.

AN EGYPTIAN BANQUET was a vibrant and colourful affair. Guests were greeted on arrival with gifts of garlands of flowers and cones made of perfumed grease that they wore on their heads. They sniffed at intoxicating mandrake fruits, and as they ate and drank were entertained by acrobatic female dancers who have provided some of the liveliest – and most erotic – images in Egyptian art. In an 18th-dynasty scene from the tomb of Nebamun at West Thebes, for example, two young girls gyrate naked except for the bead girdles around the hips, while female accompanists urge them on with hand-clapping and music from a double flute. The women shake their quivering tresses with such vitality that

TATTOOED LADY **A musician with a tattoo of the god Bes on her thigh.**

their heads turn to face the viewer – a rare phenomenon in Egyptian art, which normally shows only profiles. Another tomb painting of the same period depicts a dancing girl performing a graceful back bend, with the mass of her hair tumbling in a wavy black cataract to the floor. The tossing of the hair clearly played an important element in Egyptian dance.

In Egypt, there seems to have been no clear distinction between dancing and acrobatics. The girls in the paintings are seen shimmying, cartwheeling, spinning, tossing one another through the air and doing somersaults. Routines like these certainly required training, and a class of professional dancing girls is referred to in the records. They were

A NOSE FOR ENJOYMENT

Smell was an important sense to the Egyptians. The scribes decried any trade that involved 'stink'. Dinner-party guests wore perfume, held lotus blooms to their noses and sniffed mandrake roots. In the temples, people inhaled the incense used in religious ritual. Altogether, the nose was such a prized organ among the Egyptians that its hieroglyph not only stood for 'smell' but for 'taste', 'enjoy' and 'take pleasure in'.

The grease cone was surely one of the oddest fashion accessories of all time. Worn by guests at Egyptian banquets, it comprised a solid cone of perfumed animal fat that was placed on the head. As the room heated up, the cone melted to shed its fragrant substance over the wearer.

was certainly known in ancient Egypt, and the Egyptian Museum of Turin possesses an exceptionally frank pictorial manuscript depicting encounters between a middle-aged man and a young woman. Saucy captions accompany the vignettes, such as 'Let me make it nice for you', and 'Oh, you wicked man!' The client is comically bald and unshaven. The young woman is naked but for a hip girdle much like those worn by the dancing girls in the tomb paintings. Indeed, one of the captions describes her as a servant of Hathor.

The dancing girls were not, however, a wholly despised class. Troupes of musicians and dancers were attached to the temples as well as to royal and private households, and in the New Kingdom they were supervised by women who held the title *weret khener* ('great one of the troupe of musical

under the protection of Hathor, the goddess of sexuality associated with music and dance. The god Bes also had a role to play, for in the New Kingdom, dancers, musicians and serving girls had his image tattooed on their thighs as a good-luck charm.

SERVANTS OF HATHOR

It seems likely that the young women who performed in the name of the love goddess offered more than straightforward entertainment. Prostitution

DINNER GUESTS Banqueting ladies with perfumed cones on their heads sniff the fragrance of lotus flowers while servants offer wine.

MUSIC LOVERS Wealthy Egyptians delighted in the sensuous music provided by bands of female players.

performers'). This post was held by the wives of very high officials. Most dancing troupes were exclusively female, although male singers and musicians feature occasionally. The men of Egypt had their own dances, including specialised pieces for military occasions, but they performed separately from the women. Close as Egyptian husbands and wives were, there is no evidence of couples dancing in pairs.

Hired dwarfs and pygmies also capered before the banquet guests. The Egyptians had a special fondness

for them, and African pygmies were particularly prized for their dancing skills. The 6th-dynasty boy pharaoh, Neferkare Pepy II, awaited the arrival of a dancing pygmy from Nubia with an eagerness that is captured in his instructions to the leader of the expedition: 'Hurry and bring with you this pygmy to delight the heart. When he goes down into the ship, get worthy men to be around him on deck, lest he fall into the water.'

Dwarfs were relatively common in Egypt – the skeletons of several dozen dwarfs have been

THE DEMON DRINK

IN THE LAMENT OF IPUWER a 13th-dynasty official grieves over the disorder of Egypt in his own day, comparing it with happier times that have been lost. Yet it is good, he says, when boats can sail south without being robbed, when people can go about unmolested. It is good when men's hands build pyramids, when pools are dug and plantations made with trees for the gods. 'Yet it is good, when men are drunk, when they drink Miit and their hearts are happy'. The last sentiment strikes the modern ear as a curious one for a sage to express. But it made sense to the Egyptians for whom getting drunk was counted among life's pleasures. Intoxication was a state sacred to the goddess Hathor. At banquets, the guests drank in copious quantities. 'Give me eighteen cups of wine, for I should love to drink to drunkenness, my inside is as dry as straw', someone cries in a tomb painting caption. To save fuss, guests sometimes drank wine through straws direct from the jar. And the consequences of this intemperance are evident, in images of men and women being sick into a bowl proffered by servants, while neighbours comfort them amid the roistering.

Tolerant as the Egyptians were of heavy drinking, however, excess was not always approved. The scribes, in particular, attacked students who neglected their studies and wasted their talents through overindulgence. Here, the author of the *Satire on Trades* lambastes a young miscreant in terms that capture for all time his disgust at youthful dissipation.

I am told that you have abandoned writing
and whirl around in pleasures;
that you go from street to street,
and it reeks of beer wherever you quit.
Beer drives the people away,
it causes your soul to wander...

You are sitting in public houses,
surrounded by whores;
you sit in front of the girl, drenched in ointment,
a wreath of flowers around your neck,
drumming on your belly.
You stumble and fall flat on your face,
smeared with dirt.

TIPPLER A Nubian sips wine by a straw from the jar in this 18th-dynasty scene. A servant assists him, while his Egyptian wife looks on.

discovered, and they are represented in paintings and statuary. Besides entertaining the guests at banquets, dwarfs in the royal household had special functions such as making jewellery and looking after the pharaoh's food and his pets.

Between the lively dances a harpist, male or female, might entertain the guests with song. Harps were in use under the Old Kingdom, and the Egyptians' examples so closely resemble those of the ancient Sumerians that one must have influenced the other (it is not clear which of them can claim credit for the invention). The strings of the harp were pegged down at the neck and attached to the sound box by a suspension rod, secured by an adjustable cord to change the tone. The blind harpist was a familiar figure in ancient Egypt. Since musical notation had not been invented at this time, blindness was not a particular disadvantage – it was certainly less

WOMEN'S TRIO A tomb painting from Thebes depicts harp, long-necked lute and tambourine.

problematic to a musician than to many other tradesmen.

A fine Harpist's Song is inscribed in the 18th-dynasty tomb of King Intef, urging the carefree enjoyment of life. Its theme is an eternal one: take your pleasure while you can, for death comes sooner than you think. According to the Greek historian, Herodotus, this melancholy reflection was drummed home at Egyptian banquets when the host sometimes brought out a carved wooden mummy to remind the guests of their mortality while enjoying life's delights.

Vocalists normally sang to a single instrument, but small orchestras played for the dancers, using drums and tambourines to spur them on, and rhythmic clapping also helped to whip up excitement. For additional percussion the Egyptians possessed castanets in bone and ivory, and an ecstatic caption from the tomb painting of a nobleman called Sonebi evokes the frenzy they inspired:

> *Exalted is Hathor, she of love!*
> *O castanets! castanets!*
> *She is exalted on this free day!*
> *On this free day, O Sonebi!*
> *O castanets!*

Clappers, rattles, cymbals and bells all had particular uses in religion as well as in entertainment, especially the hand rattle known as the *sistrum*. This was a very distinctive Egyptian instrument, sometimes decorated with a head of the goddess Hathor. Strung with wires on which hung metal strips, the *sistrum* could be shaken lightly for a soothing effect or fiercely for an agitated clashing.

CEREMONIAL HARP The crowned head of the pharaoh adorns this five-string harp of the New Kingdom.

TRAVELLERS' TALES

For a more tranquil form of entertainment, leisured Egyptians played board games on beautifully ornamented sets. In fact, such was their enthusiasm for some games that chequerboards were marked out on the pavements.

INSTRUMENTS OF DELIGHT

AT FESTIVAL TIMES in ancient Egypt a wealthy man's villa echoed to sounds of drumming and dancing feet. A lively percussion section set the rhythm, and the ensemble playing for banquet guests might include any of three stringed instruments. The harp was a particular favourite, and the Egyptians also possessed a long-necked lute and a seven-string lyre. Wind instruments included splendid trumpets – a pair in gold and silver was found in Tutankhamun's tomb – but these were chiefly for military or religious use. At banquets, the reed flute, with three to five finger holes, was more likely to be heard. The flute had an ancient pedigree, dating back to prehistoric times in Egypt, when it was played by blowing through the nose. In later times, the focus switched to the mouth and the wind section came to encompass metal flutes and a reeded clarinet that is still known in Egypt under the name of *zummara*. More unusual was an oboe with a double reed that was normally played by a pair of women (one supplied a drone while the other played the melody).

Since the Egyptians never developed written notation we can only guess at the sound of their music. However, the nature of their instruments suggests that it was similar to the traditional sounds heard in modern Arab villages. The ancient Egyptians probably employed a seven-note scale, for this was adopted by the ancient Greeks, who took much of their musical theory from the ancient Middle East. The influence of the Egyptians was transmitted, in particular, through Pythagoras, who studied in Egyptian and Mesopotamian temples in the 6th century BC.

They enjoyed reading, too. One favourite tale was the *Story of Sinuhe*, set during the Middle Kingdom, which describes the adventures of a royal servant who flees Egypt for Syria. In exile he becomes a great man, but cannot be happy for, in true Egyptian fashion, he cannot conceive of contentment in any place outside the Nile valley. As an old man he is permitted to return home. Shedding his heavy foreign garments for the cool delights of Egyptian linen, Sinuhe returns with great honour to a magnificent villa. He finds his ultimate satisfaction, however, in the prospect of a grand tomb burial with all the Egyptian trimmings.

The *Story of Sinuhe* was regarded as a classic, and passages were often given to schoolboys to copy out and memorise. It also contains a tale of combat between the hero and a Syrian champion that parallels the Biblical account of David and Goliath. Another Egyptian narrative, *The Tale of the Two Brothers*, includes an episode reminiscent of the Biblical story of Potiphar's wife, where an innocent man is punished through the accusations of a scorned woman. Many other such parallels occur. At the

SNAKE GAME A gaming board of alabaster with ivory inlay, used for the Serpent Game, *mehen*.

height of Egypt's greatness there was close contact with Palestine, and traffic passed incessantly between the two countries. Though it is conceivable that the Hebrews influenced the Egyptians, it is also quite possible that the stream of information flowed the other way, and that Egypt's more extensive collections of narrative and anecdote found their way into the Old Testament.

Egyptian tales clearly influenced the literature of later peoples. One travel story, called *The Shipwrecked Sailor,* includes features that turn up in both Homer's *Odyssey* and the story of Sindbad the sailor in *The Thousand and One Nights*. The location is an enchanted island inhabited by a gigantic snake that is covered in gold scales and has eyebrows of lapis lazuli. Bearded like a god, the fire-breathing monster has the power of human speech, and the sailor is naturally terrified of it. His fears, though, are eventually allayed when the snake becomes friendly, showers him with gifts and reassures him that he will one day reach his home town, where (a vital detail) he will be buried with the proper rites when he dies.

The literate Egyptian read stories on papyrus rolls or on *ostraca* (broken pieces of earthenware). For the multitudes who could not read, there was the storyteller. Folk tales were rich in supernatural events, and a cycle called *Tales of Wonder* has survived, describing the miracles performed by great magicians of the

A Craze for Board Games

FOR EGYPTIAN men and women alike, board games were something of a passion. By far the most popular was *senet* ('passing'), played on a board divided into three rows of ten squares. The set might be made of anything from clay, stone or wood to faience or ivory, and some took the form of a rectangular box with the board marked out on the top, and drawers at each end for the pieces. The aim was to get one's own pieces off the board while stopping the opponent from doing the same. Players determined the number of squares they could move by throwing marked sticks, or a knucklebone called an *astralgus* (dice were not known under the pharaohs). Pieces followed a zigzag path along the board, and if a counter found its way barred it had to go back and start again.

Senet was being played in Egypt even before the coming of the pharaohs, and furnished a common

motif in tomb paintings. Typically, the tomb owner is shown sitting at a *senet* board, facing an invisible opponent, hoping to 'pass' safely through to the afterlife.

Sets were portable, and some boards were reversible, with the underside marked out for another popular

POPULAR PASTIME
This beautifully crafted board for playing *senet* displays the three rows of ten squares.

TOMB PAINTING The lord Hunefer, seated at a *senet* board, pits his wits against an unseen adversary.

game called *taw*, or 'twenty squares'. Here the squares were laid out in three rows of four, twelve and four, but the aim was similar to *senet* in that the player strove to get pieces off the board while blocking the adversary. *Taw* was brought to Egypt from the Near East by the Hyksos invaders who overran the country at the end of the Middle Kingdom.

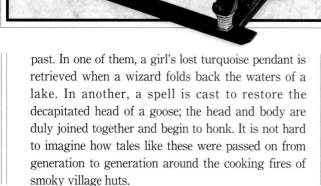

past. In one of them, a girl's lost turquoise pendant is retrieved when a wizard folds back the waters of a lake. In another, a spell is cast to restore the decapitated head of a goose; the head and body are duly joined together and begin to honk. It is not hard to imagine how tales like these were passed on from generation to generation around the cooking fires of smoky village huts.

But the reading classes took pleasure in more sober works too, such as those reflecting on the state of the world. One particularly gloomy example is the *Admonitions of Ipuwer*, written during the years of turmoil that came between the Old and Middle Kingdoms in the 22nd century BC. In it the author regrets the overthrow of the established order, lamenting that the poor have become rich and that former men of property have become paupers. The world has been turned upside down, and the consequences are disastrous:

Look, great and small say: 'I wish I were dead.'
Little children say: 'He should not have made me
live!'
Look, children of nobles are dashed against walls,
infants are cast on high ground. . .

Another notable work, *The Protests of the Eloquent Peasant*, was written during the same age of upheaval. The peasant in question is robbed by a well-connected gentleman and appeals to the pharaoh's High Steward to intervene on his behalf. The official is eventually won over by the peasant's eloquence and after hearing nine appeals duly restores the man's stolen property. The importance of the work

---

THE WORLD'S FIRST PLAY

Although Egypt had no commercial theatre, the country has been credited with staging the world's first recorded play. This was a ritual drama depicting the murder and resurrection of the god Osiris. From very early times it was performed outside the gate of the temple in the ancient city of Abydos.

---

lies in its critique of social injustice in Egypt. It is extremely unusual in any ancient literature for an author to take up the voice of a working man against his supposed betters. At one point, the 'eloquent' peasant attacks the High Steward's own wealth. 'You are selfish . . . you steal . . .' he complains. 'Your portion is in your house and your belly full, while the corn measure brims over and overflows, so that its excess perishes on the ground.'

The Eloquent Peasant is exceptional in the vehemence of its tone. But a respect for humble folk is also exhibited in Egypt's so-called 'wisdom literature' – collections of wise sayings addressed by one or another elderly sage to the young of his day. These books of instruction were a common form of reading matter and gave clear moral guidance to educated Egyptians. They mostly stressed the values of justice, restraint and humility – important for officials who were operating in the confines of an authoritarian society. One such work, the *Teaching of Amenemope,* for example, recommends fair treatment for the poor, for widows, for the blind and other similar disadvantaged groups. There may have been a huge difference in wealth between Egypt's leisured classes and the mass of the peasantry, but public morality was quite clear in recommending just treatment for all.

FABULOUS BEASTS **Three creatures of Egyptian legend, sketched on a 3000-year-old limestone fragment.**

OUTDOOR ENTERTAINMENTS

Crowds of common folk cheered as wrestlers grappled in the sand. Noblemen hunted wild game

with their chariots and hounds and pursued fish and waterfowl in the marshes. All thrilled at the

pageantry of the annual religious festivals.

HOLIDAYS provided everyone with an opportunity to let off steam. The royal workmen at Deir el-Medina had one day off in ten, and there were additional holidays scattered throughout the calendar, associated with royal occasions, with local deities or with fixed points in the calendar. The Egyptians celebrated the New Year, for example, and the Harvest. Flood time was the season of the great religious festivals, when images of the gods were paraded in colourful procession through the countryside. Festivities often lasted for weeks, and the most spectacular were the flood-time celebrations for Amun. Priests carried the god's effigy from his shrine at Karnak aboard a sacred barge that was towed up the Nile to Luxor. The god was lodged at the temple there for nearly a month before returning to Karnak. The peasants were granted a holiday during the festival and vast crowds cheered from the riverbank as Amun processed up and down.

Religion furnished life with much of its grandest pageantry. The ancient city of Abydos was the main centre for the worship of Osiris and here, it was said, the souls of the dead came from all over the country to gather at the tomb of the deity. The city was also the goal of an immense popular pilgrimage. All Egyptians hoped to visit Abydos to attend a dramatic annual re-enactment of the Osiris myth.

THE LOVE OF THE CHASE

Rumbustious boating contests were staged on the Nile, where teams of men with poles tilted at one another to knock opponents out of the water. Though the Egyptians had nothing comparable to the Olympic Games of the ancient Greeks, it is clear that a variety of athletic events were known to them. Images of high-jumping and long-jumping have survived, and running was regarded as an important activity. In the 30th year of his reign (and every third

SPORTING LIFE The noble pastime of ostrich hunting is portrayed on this goldwork from Tutankhamun's tomb.

Fighting Fit Wrestling and stick-fencing provided training for military life, and also entertained Egyptian crowds.

year after that), the people celebrated the pharaoh's continued good health in a ceremony known as the *sed*. During the festivities the king was supposed to demonstrate his prowess with a long-distance run. Originally the route of this run went around the walls of the city of Memphis, but in later times it was shortened.

The Egyptians loved to watch wrestling, a sport shown in many paintings, with varieties of hand holds and throws. Bouts of wrestling seem to have been mounted among the entertainment at feasts,

along with music, song and dance. Weightlifting, bare-fist boxing and fencing with sticks were practised too – all pastimes with particular benefits for soldiers. They were, however, chiefly for the lower orders. Archery was considered a much more suitable activity for noblemen. After the chariot became fashionable, Egyptian kings and princes got the taste for archery tournaments in which they rode at top speed, loosing arrows at copper targets. The pharaoh Amenhotep II had his expertise celebrated for future generations on a carved stone relief depicting him in

THE PLEASURES OF FISHING AND FOWLING

A PASTORAL LYRIC, probably composed during the 12th dynasty, describes the pleasures of a hunting expedition in pursuit of wildfowl and fish in the marshes – the kind enjoyed by many Egyptian lords. Although the papyrus is fragmentary, it appears that the speaker is a town-dweller expressing regret for the lost charms of his rural boyhood:

❝ A happy day when we go down to the marsh, that we may snare birds and catch many fishes in the two waters . . . a happy day on which we give to everybody and the marsh goddess is propitious. We shall trap birds and shall light a brazier to Sobek . . .

ON THE RIVERBANK A hippo looks on as a man goes netting on the Nile.

I settle at the ford and make ready for myself a screen after I have fastened my bait. I am in the cool breeze whilst my fishes are in the sun. I kill at every thrust, there is no stop for my spear. I make bundles of bulti-fish . . .

I go down to the lake. Staves are on my shoulder, my poles and two and one-fifth cubits of rope under my arm. I attend to tugging at five cubits of draw rope by hand. The water is sluggish. The thick cloth* which the hand holds, we see it fall after we have heard the quacking of the pool's birds. We snare them in the net. ❞

A signal cloth waved to tell hunters when to pull the clapnet shut.

---

action. He is said to have possessed a bow so sturdy that only he was capable of bending it.

In prehistoric times, hunting made a vital contribution to the Egyptians' diet, and long after the people became farmers it survived as a sport of kings and courtiers. Egyptian nobles were often depicted in their tombs hunting in the desert. To spear a wild bull or hippopotamus was to display more than courage and skill. It represented the triumph of order and life over chaos and death.

Out in the desert, gazelles and antelopes were a favourite quarry. However, imperial conquests under the New Kingdom opened up exciting new territory for keen sportsmen. Thutmose III boasted that he had killed 120 elephants in northern Syria, and he hunted a rhinoceros in Sudan. Not all hunting expeditions ended in mass killing. Traps and lassos allowed huntsmen to bring back animals for display and for breeding purposes.

In the marshes, Egyptian lords enjoyed the thrill of stalking hippopotamuses. The noblemen pursued their quarry in groups, moving on papyrus boats through the reeded swamps. On sighting a hippo they hurled harpoon-like spears. When the weapons hit their target the shaft broke off, leaving the spearhead embedded in the creature's hide, attached to a stout rope. Even when hit by several spears, a full-size hippo would have put up a tremendous fight, roaring and thrashing amid the tangle of ropes, so that wise hunters kept a safe distance until the monster was exhausted and could be drawn to the bank.

Fishing and fowling offered quieter pleasures in the marshes. Tomb scenes often depict Egyptian lords hunting wildfowl from boats, usually hurling a curved throwing stick, like a boomerang, to break the bird's neck. They are also shown spearing fish. In the paintings, the noble sportsmen have wives, children, servants and even pets alongside them, as if hunting in the marshes was an outing for the whole family.

This may not have been the case, however. Women did not normally accompany men in their sporting activities, and scholars have detected various religious references in the tomb pictures. It may be that the family's mastery of the marshland wildlife was intended to represent a symbolic mastery of fertile primordial forces, having meanings connected with rebirth. Whether the family pictures are symbolic or realistic, however, it is evident that hunting in the marshes was considered an idyllic form of recreation.

MIND, BODY AND SPIRIT

A jackal-headed priest holds a mummy case upright in the ceremony
known as the Opening of the Mouth. Egyptian burial rites are famous for their
mystery and complexity, but the priests were not only preoccupied with the Beyond.
The temples were at the heart of extensive communities bustling with activity,
and were also great centres of learning where skills of astronomy,
medicine and mathematics were pioneered.

REALM OF THE SPIRIT

'I am the Lord of Fire who lives on Truth!' cries Egypt's creator god in an ancient text.

For the people of the Nile, existence was animated by vast, unseen spiritual forces,

presiding over life and death alike.

AT THE BURIAL of an Egyptian official called Ani, a priest waves a censer to load the air with perfume, while servants bring rich grave offerings to the tomb. One attendant carries the foreleg from a sacrificial calf. Nearby, groups of women wail and beat their breasts in mourning. The coffin is raised upright before a table heaped with gifts, and Ani's grief-stricken widow falls to her knees before the encased body of her lord. A priest starts to read from a papyrus, murmuring a sacred incantation to open a path for Ani's spirit into the realm of the dead. The ceremony is called the Opening of the Mouth, and is designed to revive the mummified man's senses so that he can eat, drink and speak in the next world. Some of the priests standing by are clad in panther skins. One wears a jackal mask.

To an outsider, perhaps, all religious ceremony has a quality of mystery. But the Egyptian death rites, with their sacred spells, humanoid coffins and animal-headed priests, convey a sense of strangeness like no other. The scene described above is the burial of a relatively humble scribe as depicted on an 18th-

THE PRELUDE Ani's widow weeps by her husband's coffin as cattle draw it by sled to his place of burial.

dynasty papyrus, and it followed an oft-repeated formula. In the Opening of the Mouth ritual, a favourite sacrificial offering was the leg of a calf with the blood still spurting from its veins. The jackal-masked impersonator of Anubis, the god of embalming, and the women lamenting were key figures in the proceedings. The propped-up mummy case traditionally faced south and was often adorned by the attendants with a special headdress and a necklace of flowers. Balls of salt were offered to it for ritual purification; the lips on the coffin face were moistened with cow's milk, and cosmetics were applied to the eyes. A priest would then touch the coffin's mouth with an *adze*, which resembled the constellation of the Great Bear in shape, in order to awaken the dead person's senses.

Only when the rites had been fully observed were the coffin and possessions of the deceased taken to the burial chamber. Funeral preparations lasted 70 days – a limbo period corresponding to the length of time during which the brightest star in the Egyptian firmament, Sirius, the 'Dog Star', appeared to die by dipping below the horizon. The 70-day rule was applied to lords and commoners alike, though the ceremonies for a great pharaoh were more elaborate.

DANCE OF DEATH The Egyptians grieved noisily. Here, mourning women dance and beat tambourines.

A correct burial was every Egyptian's dream – in a passage from the literary classic, *The Tale of Sinuhe*, the hero is lured back to Egypt by the promise of a splendid funeral with all the trimmings:

> *A funeral procession is made for you on the day*
> *of burial; the mummy case is of gold, its head of*
> *lapis lazuli. The sky is above you as you lie in the*
> *hearse, oxen drawing you, musicians going*
> *before you. The dance of the* mww-*dancers is*
> *done at the door of your tomb; the offering-list is*
> *read to you; sacrifice is made before your*
> *offering-table. You shall not die abroad! You*
> *shall not be wrapped in the skin of a ram to*
> *serve as your coffin.*

EYEWITNESS

DEATH IS...

A 12TH-DYNASTY TEXT known as the *Dialogue between a Man Tired of Life and his Soul* describes both the agony and the blessedness of dying, reflecting the Egyptians' pre-occupation with death and the afterlife. In the final speech the writer comes to terms with his own mortality and extols death as a means of fulfilment after a life of struggle and uncertainty:

> *Death is before me today*
> *like a sick man's recovery,*
> *like going outside after confinement.*
>
> *Death is before me today*
> *like the scent of myrrh,*
> *like sitting under a sail on a windy day.*
>
> *Death is before me today*
> *like the scent of lotuses,*
> *like sitting on the shore of drunkenness.*
>
> *Death is before me today*
> *like a well trodden path,*
> *like a man's coming home from war.*
>
> *Death is before me today*
> *like the opening of the sky,*
> *like a man's grasping what he did not know.*
>
> *Death is before me today*
> *like a man's longing to see home*
> *having spent many years abroad.*

Fantastic energy was lavished on royal tomb-building and furnishing, and the prior preparations could last over decades. Kings and courtiers often chose their own burial sites when they were young

HEART AND SOUL

Tomb offerings and bandaged mummies might appear macabre relics, but they testify to an abiding faith in the immortal soul.

A BIRD-LIKE SPIRIT with feathered wings and human head was often depicted in tomb paintings soaring above the coffin of a dead man. This was the *ba*, which was said to emerge from the body at death and could choose any shape that took its fancy. The *ba* was able to leave a tomb and revisit the dead man's haunts in the mortal world. It was also the *ba* that ascended to heaven to join the entourage of the sun god, descending with it at dusk into the underworld.

The *ba* was not, however, the only spirit of the deceased, for the Egyptians believed an individual's being to have many aspects. The primary soul was the *ka*, an earthbound entity said to dwell in every individual. After death it remained with the mummy, taking nourishment from the daily offerings brought by relatives or priests.

In life, the heart was considered to be the seat of the *ka*, and an organ of much greater significance than the brain. While the latter was discarded during mummification, the embalmers took care to leave the heart in place, for it would be needed when the dead person faced his or her day of judgment. This was an occasion of immense significance

THE BEST EMBALMER

Egypt's hot, dry climate did a better job at preserving the dead than the skills of the priests. Sealed in his gold coffin, Tutankhamun's corpse was almost destroyed by the embalmer's oils. The prehistoric people of Naqada were buried in the warm sand of Upper Egypt, but their bodies have survived nearly twice as long.

to all Egyptians, when the gods decided whether an individual was fit to be gathered into the company of the blessed. The Judgment of the Dead is often portrayed in tomb scenes: typically, the heart of the deceased is balanced against an ostrich feather symbolising the deeds of their lifetime. Those found wanting risked being cast into the fearful darkness of extinction, represented in paintings by the jaws of a crocodile-headed monster. Maat, the goddess of truth, presided over the tribunal, and the anguish with which the Egyptians awaited judgment is vividly evoked in this prayer from the *Book of the Dead*:

'O my heart which I had from my mother! O my heart which I had from my mother! O my heart of different ages! Do not stand up as a witness against me, do not be opposed to me in the tribunal, do not be hostile to me in the presence of the Keeper of the Balance, for you are my ka *which was in my body, the protector who made my members hale. Go forth to the happy place whereto we speed; do not make my name stink to the Entourage who make men. Do not tell lies about me in the presence of the god; it is indeed well that you should hear!'*

JUDGMENT DAY The gods weigh a soul on the scales of justice to determine the dead person's fate in the afterlife.

SOUL TAKES WING A bird-like spirit known as the *ba* was believed to soar from the body at the time of death.

men, and they spent much of their adult lives gathering up the treasures that were to accompany them into the afterlife. Lords watched with keen interest as work on their sepulchre progressed, and would often take their wives and children on a trip to the site to see how things were going.

CLOSE ENCOUNTERS WITH THE GODS

The Egyptian concern with the afterlife bequeathed the world the riches of Tutankhamun's tomb as well as the colossal architecture of the pyramids, built as monumental graves for dead kings. But it indicates more than a preoccupation with death alone. It speaks of an extraordinary faith in the enduring power of the spirit.

For Egyptian believers, the whole fabric of everyday life was threaded with magic. Humans, birds, animals, reptiles, fishes, insects, flowers . . . all were manifestations of a divine essence that flowed into everything. The godhead could ebb from one form and seep into another, so that spells were cast at the time of a man's death to transform him into a falcon of gold, into a crocodile or a phoenix. At the funeral of the official, Ani, a spell was cast to transform him into a lotus: 'I am this pure lotus which went forth from the sunshine, which is the nose of Re; I have descended that I may seek it for Horus, for I am the pure one who issued from the fen.' Ani hoped for reunion with the sun god Re, and the lotus was a flower symbolising Re's daily rebirth.

Not all encounters with the world of the spirit were agreeable. Among the Egyptians, any misfortune, from a headache to a national famine, might be attributed to a supernatural agency, and people lived in terror of evil spirits and of the gods' displeasure. Coping with the shining yet menacing universe of the spirit was essentially a job for the priests, who carried out set rituals on behalf of the population. Ordinary Egyptians were not allowed to enter into the sacred precincts, and they were barred from the daily rites of the great state gods.

Over 2000 deities were worshipped in ancient Egypt. Some were state gods, some were concerned with matters of daily importance, such as childbirth and health, and others governed the realms of the dead. Some gods were organised into families and

> ### DID YOU KNOW?
>
> The Egyptians had doctors for different parts of the body. One court physician was doctor to the pharaoh's eyes, doctor to the king's belly and 'shepherd of the king's anus'.
>
> The Egyptians seriously underestimated the brain as an organ. They believed that the heart controlled thinking and that the sole purpose of the brain was to pass mucus to the nose.

were believed to have ruled on earth before the pharaohs. The sun god Re created two children, Shu and his sister-wife Tefnut, who represented moisture, from which all living things came. Their children were the earth god Geb and the sky goddess Nut, whose divine union produced Isis, Osiris, Seth and Nephthys. Osiris 'invented' civilisation, and the pharaoh was considered his heir.

One reason for the extraordinary number of gods was that the ancient local deities worshipped in different parts of the country were still revered when Egypt was united (c.3150). Regional loyalties remained strong throughout Egyptian history, so that as a city rose to prominence at a given period so too did its favourite deity. Re, the sun god of Heliopolis ('Sun City', now situated in a modern suburb of Cairo), became a state god in the 5th dynasty and his influence steadily increased through the ages. His priests showed considerable resourcefulness. When the city of Thebes rose to supremacy, so too did its obscure local god, Amun, and in response the priests at Heliopolis cheerfully attached the name of their own god to that of Amun and worshipped him as Amun-Re. It was a move very much in the spirit of Egyptian religion, which permitted all kinds of overlapping roles. Dogma did not bother the Egyptians much. The key element in religion was (continued on p.128)

GIFT FOR A GODDESS A 19th-dynasty silver figurine shows a pharaoh making an offering before Maat, goddess of truth.

PRESERVED FOR ETERNITY

MUMMIFIED FACES of the ancient Egyptians survive as beautiful yet macabre relics of a civilisation. Egyptian embalmers were secretive about their arts and left no accounts to describe mummification. Present-day knowledge is based chiefly on the study of mummies themselves, and on the writings of Herodotus.

The dead person's body was removed for ritual washing before being carried to the embalming workshop. There, the priests first disposed of the deceased's brain by puncturing the membrane with a hook inserted through the nostrils. The brain liquefied on contact with the air and drained out when the head was turned to one side.

Next, an incision was made in the abdomen in order to withdraw the intestines, which were deposited in alabaster jars. The heart was left in place because it would be needed on the dead person's Day of Judgment. The body and cavity in the abdomen were dried with crystals of natron, a compound of sodium carbonate and bicarbonate that stopped the corpse rotting. Then the skin was daubed with scented oils to restore its suppleness, and a fluid resin was poured into the brain cavity, where it later solidified. The body was cleansed with scented palm wine and fumigated with incense, and the innards were packed with a dry material such as linen or straw. The body was then wrapped in a linen winding sheet, with lucky charms

SARCOPHAGUS Mummies were placed in a stone or terracotta coffin bearing the deceased's likeness and decorated with ritual motifs.

and scarabs being slipped into the folds. The wrapped figure was deposited in a wooden coffin or stone sarcophagus and returned to

the grieving family ready for the Opening of the Mouth ceremony.

There were cheaper procedures that amounted, in the cases of the humbler citizens, to little more than washing the body, drying it with natron and bundling it up in coarse cloth. Destined for a communal grave, it might nonetheless be interred with a few morsels of food and perhaps some simple utensils.

CROCODILE MUMMY The Egyptians preserved animals as well as humans.

A GALLERY OF GODS

Horned, maned, hawk-faced and crocodile-headed gods all marched side by side in Egypt's grand parade of deities.

THE EGYPTIANS worshipped a multitude of gods. Many were local deities at first, but were absorbed into a system of belief that permitted overlapping roles. The priests evolved a creation myth and a family tree to explain how some of the main gods and goddesses were related. In the limitless darkness there existed a primeval ocean called Nun, out of which rose the sun god Re, a supreme being who spat out the elements of air and moisture. They in turn gave birth to the earth god, Geb, and the sky goddess, Nut. And out of their union came four children: Osiris, Isis, Seth and Nephthys. Some of the main gods and their attributes were:

RE   The sun god and lord of creation. From his centre of worship at Heliopolis he rose to become a national deity. By day Re traversed the sky in his sun boat; at night he disappeared into the underworld. Worshippers hoped for reunion with Re in the afterlife. He was pictured with a falcon's head (like Horus) and a sun disc.

AMUN   Originally a fertility god worshipped in Thebes, Amun became one of Egypt's national deities. As a sky god, he fused with Re, and became Amun-Re, the king of the gods.

OSIRIS   The god of death and rebirth, associated with the growth and decay of vegetation. In winter he was thought to disappear with the crops into the underworld, and he had a special role as god of the dead.

ISIS   The sister and wife of Osiris. In mythology she reconstructed Osiris after his murder by his brother Seth. Ordinary folk worshipped Isis as a maternal and protective goddess, with many healing powers. She was often represented holding the infant Horus, and sometimes shown (like Hathor) with cow's horns.

NEPHTHYS   The sister and bosom companion of Isis. Nephthys was the wife of the evil Seth, but when this malign god murdered Osiris her sympathies lay with the heart-broken Isis.

SETH   The brother and murderer of Osiris. A sky god in origin, Seth was said to have killed his brother and so came to represent evil and chaotic forces. Offerings were made to him nonetheless, for he was Lord of the Red Land, or desert, and the ruler of droughts and storms.

HORUS   The son of Osiris and Isis, he was portrayed as a falcon god. Believing themselves to be offspring of the gods, the pharaohs saw themselves as living incarnations of Horus and capable of soaring with him to the sun. People wore Eye of Horus amulets to ward off the evil eye.

HATHOR   The goddess of love, happiness, music – and inebriation. Portrayed as a cow, or with a head-

Re   Amun   Osiris   Isis   Nephthys

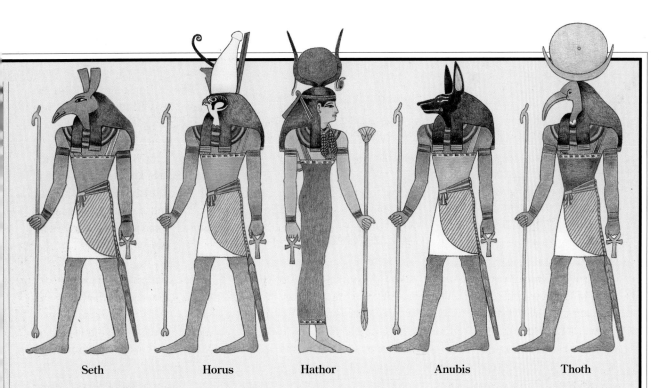

Seth   Horus   Hathor   Anubis   Thoth

gear of cow's horns, this popular deity embodied female sexuality and fertility. Hathor was the patron of dancing girls, and was invoked by women during childbirth.

ANUBIS   The jackal-headed god of embalming, who admitted the dead to the underworld. Priests officiating at the Opening of the Mouth ceremony wore a jackal-headed Anubis mask. According to one account, Anubis was the offspring of the gods Nephthys and Osiris.

THOTH   The god of learning, Thoth kept the gods' records and was credited with the invention of writing and mathematics. Thoth was the patron of scribes, and his major cult centre was at Khmunu.

PTAH   The local god of Memphis, and among the most ancient and prominent of Egypt's deities. He was named supreme god at the time when Egypt was first unified, and was credited by his priests with the world's creation. In

later times he was known as the god of craftsmen.

KHNUM   The ram-headed god of the cataract region of the Nile, Khnum was said to control the river's annual flood. The ram symbolised procreativity, and the priests in Khnum's temple at Esnu taught that the god was humankind's creator.

SOBEK   The crocodile-headed solar god. His centre of worship was at the oasis city of Shedet (also known as Crocodilopolis) in the Faiyum district of northern Egypt, where there were water reservoirs vital to the whole country. Fishermen made offerings to Sobek to propitiate the fearsome reptile god.

SAKHMET   The lioness goddess, whose name meant 'The Powerful One', was a ferocious war goddess employed by the vengeful sun god against the human race. She also caused – and cured – epidemics.

Ptah   Khnum   Sobek   Sakhmet

ritual: the priests' ceremonies, sacrifices and magic incantations were thought essential for the orderly running of the Egyptian world.

The god-like pharaoh exercised supreme authority over ritual. After him the High Priest, who was chosen for the job by the pharaoh himself, governed the religious life of the people – an awesome responsibility. In the New Kingdom, one of the greatest temples – that of Amun at Karnak – was staffed by an army of 81 322 people who busied themselves about the estate's fields, herds, workshops, archives, granaries, stores and wharves. There were 421 362 head of livestock, 433 orchards, 65 villages and 83 ships; the arable land sprawled over 924 sq miles (2393 sq km), and a visitor to the temple would have seen the farmers of the temple estates ploughing or harvesting according to the season, cultivating vines, plucking fruit or attending to the beehives. At the riverside, temple labourers hauled shipments of building stone onto the quay. In the workshops, overseers supervised the manufacture of fine linen and golden ornaments. In the cool chambers of the temple library, its walls lined with recesses for papyrus rolls, other priests pored over manuscripts of precious learning. By night, standing on the very roofs of the sacred buildings, astronomer-priests studied the movements of the heavenly bodies.

At the heart of the bustling community was the sacred precinct where priests performed the all-important religious services. Laymen could only enter the forecourt, and the priests themselves had to undergo ritual purification at a stone pool before they went into the inner sanctum. In the bigger temples, the sacred pool was lake-size, and on it the barque of the local deity was sailed on ceremonial occasions. The pool was so large that the priests had to descend a long flight of steps to reach the water, which they sprinkled over themselves both for cleansing and for contact with the primeval moisture of life.

The Daily Rite was a vital celebration, for which the priests purified themselves before dawn. Then they passed in procession through the heavy gates of an immense hall forested with stone columns, which were carved at the top with images of lotus and papyrus. Through room after room they went, burning incense to purify the air, the chambers dwindling and darkening as they advanced amid an atmosphere of deepening mystery. At last they approached the closed doors of the shrine. With great solemnity, the officiating priest broke the clay seal that had been applied to the double doors the day before. Inside the candle-lit chapel stood a shrine containing the statue of the god. And now the officiating priest began to recite a prayer, reaching out a hand to invite the god to assume his earthly form.

At this point the assistants brought forth plates of food, jugs of beer and wine, water and boxes of toiletries. Next they fed the statue, washed it, oiled its limbs, robed it in fine linen, and powdered its face

---

EYEWITNESS

THREE SPELLS

THE EGYPTIANS anticipated meeting all kinds of perils in the afterlife and took various measures to guard against them. They placed objects such as scarabs in the wrappings of the mummies and cast spells for protection. The three spells that follow are all taken from the *Book of the Dead*:

SPELL FOR DRIVING OFF A SNAKE

O Rerek-snake, take yourself off, for Geb protects me; get up, for you have eaten a mouse, which Re detests, and you have chewed the bones of a putrid cat.

SPELL FOR REPELLING A BEETLE

Begone from me, O Crooked-lips. I am Khnum, Lord of Peshu, who dispatches the words of the gods to Re, and I report affairs to their master.

SPELL FOR NOT PUTREFYING IN THE REALM OF THE DEAD

Weary, weary are the members of Osiris! They shall not be weary, they shall not putrefy, they shall not decay, they shall not swell up! May it be done to me in like manner, for I am Osiris.

TEMPLE LIFE **The public made offerings in the outer courtyard but were barred from the inner sanctum.**

dedicated to Amun, to Hathor and to Ptah. It seems that the skilled workers who comprised the community set up the shrines as places where they could drop in for worship. Some of the offerings took the form of a *stele* (carved column) inscribed with a prayer.

In their homes, the villagers of Deir el-Medina worshipped images of household gods, and busts of relations who had passed away. The Egyptians felt close to their deceased relatives, made offerings at their tombs and often addressed prayers to them, asking them to intercede with the gods on their behalf.

In this 10th-dynasty letter, a man called Merirtifi greets his dead wife in the 'west' (the land of the

MEN ONLY   A husband receives a sanctified bouquet in a temple area barred to women. Right: outside, he presents the flowers to his wife.

with rouge. The toilet was the responsibility of a priest known as the *medjty*, who as a final touch would anoint the god's forehead with a dab of oil applied with the little finger of his right hand.

BEWARE OF PTAH!

Similar services were performed at midday and at sunset, after which the god was sealed into his sanctuary for the night. The people of Egypt saw nothing of these ceremonies. But they did get opportunities to view the gods' statues at festivals, when the effigies were brought out of the temples and paraded before the public in glittering attire. Every year, the mysteries of Osiris were enacted before crowds at Abydos. Amun was paraded along the Nile in a dazzling flotilla, from Karnak to Luxor and back again.

The temple gods may only have been revealed to ordinary people at festival time, but common folk did have small shrines in which they could say prayers or make offerings all year round. At Deir el-Medina, for example, archaeologists have discovered chapels

setting sun and of death), and asks her to intercede on his behalf :

How are you? Is the west taking care of you as
*   you desire?*
Look, I am your beloved on earth,
so fight for me, intercede for my name!
I have performed all your funerary rites without
*   error.*
Drive off the illness of my limbs!
May you appear for me as a blessed one before
*   me,*
that I may see you fighting for me in a dream.

AN EGYPTIAN PRIEST ON TEMPLE DUTY

SHAVEN-HEADED AND CLAD in thin linen robes, Panefer knelt at the stone-flagged edge of the sacred pool in order to cleanse his hands and face. The dawn air was chilly and the water colder still, but the ritual ablutions had to be performed. For Panefer, as for all his companions, cleanliness was the first rule of his vocation. Cleanliness required that he be circumcised, that he be bald-headed – even that he shave off his eyebrows.

Once he was properly cleansed, Panefer joined the dignified procession of priests to take part in the morning rite of the god in his shrine. All wore white sandals and the finest linen from the temple's weaving workshop; the senior priests sported leopard-skin capes and the lector – who read the prayers in the shrine – wore a bright ribbon across his chest. Panefer, a relatively lowly priest, bore bread and cakes for the god's breakfast. These were offered to the statue every morning, but since the deity was present only in effigy, the food was not physically consumed. It would be removed from the shrine later in the day, and shared among the temple staff.

On an ordinary day, the priests locked the statue up again after the rite was completed. But today was a festival, when the god was to be taken out into the town and surrounding villages and revealed to the people. Necklaces, bracelets and amulets of gold and silver were heaped about the divine effigy. Glimmering with stones such as turquoise, carnelian and lapis lazuli, the statue was fitted into a cedarwood barque, which the priests heaved onto a stretcher. Now, with some difficulty, bearers raised the heavy barque onto their shoulders, swaying slightly as they moved out of the shrine and processed through the massive temple gates into the town.

Wild cheering greeted the cortege as it passed through the streets, with incense billowing from a bowl carried by a priest who walked at the head of the procession, drums beating, trumpets blaring and the sunlight glittering on the great effigy of the god himself. From time to time the procession came to a halt so that prayers could be uttered and offerings made. The rest also provided an opportunity for spectators to come forward from the crowd and seek a prophecy from the god. Applicants approached with great humility, asking about the health of a sick child, about their hopes for promotion, or whether they should sell their house. Some put their questions in writing, either on papyrus or on a fragment of pottery. All enquiries were put in such a way that only a yes or no answer was required. If the divine spirit moved the bearers to take a step forward, it was interpreted as a 'yes', if backwards, a 'no'.

SACRED RATTLE The sistrum was an instrument shaken in religious rites to pacify destructive forces.

MAN OF GOD Bronze figure of a shaven-headed priest, from the New Kingdom period.

All that morning the priests travelled in procession around the town. In the afternoon they boarded boats and went down the Nile to visit some of the smaller towns and villages across the river. By the evening, when they returned, Panefer was weary and all too conscious of how dusty he had become. Years of temple training had left him exceptionally fastidious. He was hungry, too, and he longed to return to the house in the temple precinct where he stayed while serving his regular turn on temple duty. Like many of his companions in the priesthood, Panefer was a married man – the priesthood did not call for celibacy (although affairs with priestesses or temple dancers were strictly forbidden) – and he lived with his wife in a house on the temple estate when not on duty.

Festival days were occasions for great celebrations, and that night the crowds jostled in the torchlit streets of the town, drinking beer and eating meat roasted on spits over open fires, as the cortege passed back through the great temple gates. The bearers returned the god to his shrine. The evening rites and ablutions were performed. And with the sounds of drumming still filling the night air, Panefer walked back to the priests' lodgings.

Pyramids and Tombs

The gigantic mounds of masonry, the fantastic, rock-cut sepulchres,

the tomb walls covered with colourful and detailed paintings . . . Egypt's tomb monuments were

more than memorials for the dead. They were machines for immortality.

NOTHING MORE POWERFULLY evokes the grandeur of Egypt and her gods than the spectacle of the gigantic pyramids. Bursting in awesome geometry from the level sands of Giza, the colossal monuments have cast their spell over generations of visitors. 'They have seen civilisations that we have never known,' wrote the 19th-century French author, Théophile Gautier, 'understood languages that we try to guess through hieroglyphics, known customs that to us seem as fantastical as a dream. They have been there so long that even the stars have changed positions in the sky.' The pyramids are so closely identified with Egyptian civilisation that it is easy to imagine that their construction was a permanent feature of daily life. In fact, pyramid-building was intermittent. The golden age, when the Giza monuments were erected, lasted for only 100 or so years under the Old Kingdom (2686-2181 BC). During the First Intermediate Period (2134-2023 BC) the practice was abandoned, and although pyramid-building was revived by some of the Middle Kingdom pharaohs (2033-1650 BC), it disappeared for good early in the New Kingdom (1570-1070 BC). Thereafter, kings chose to be buried in rock-cut tombs in the Valley of the Kings at Thebes.

'He has Kissed the Sky'

No one can say for certain why the Egyptians decided upon a pyramid shape, but it may well have reflected the primal drama of their landscape. Every year, looking out across the flood, they saw hummocks poking up and, as a result, they came to revere the mound, emerging from a watery flux, as an image of creation. The pyramid – a mound of masonry – had its base on the earth but soared towards the higher world with its promise of eternal life. It appeared in

LAST RESTING PLACE **Interior of the tomb of Sennefer, mayor of Thebes in the 18th dynasty.**

its earliest form as the Step Pyramid, the world's oldest stone monument, which was built at Saqqara by King Djoser (2668-2649 BC). The design suggests a gigantic stairway that would allow the dead king to climb heavenwards. In Djoser's monument the burial chamber was underground, but it took less than 100 years for the true pyramid to evolve, with a tomb in the heart of the structure. Instead of providing a stepped silhouette, the sides sloped at an angle to the ground, perhaps emulating the rays of the sun. The king's spirit could soar to the heavens by sunbeam or starlight, it was believed. A pyramid hymn proclaimed: 'He is no longer upon earth, he is in the sky! He rushes at the sky like a heron; he has kissed the sky like a falcon; he has leapt skyward like a grasshopper.' But the king would not abandon the

THE GREAT ENIGMA   Built around 2550 BC, the Sphinx is numbered among the ancient wonders of the world.

earth forever – he could also descend by celestial rays to reoccupy his mummified body and partake of the food offerings placed in the tomb. In the great pyramid the burial chamber lies high up in the centre, with other passages and chambers below ground level. Narrow 'air shafts' slanted upwards from the tomb to the sky. These were so orientated as to link the pharaoh's spirit with the constellation of Orion in the night sky.

HOW THE PYRAMIDS WERE BUILT

The three greatest pyramids were built at Giza in the 26th century BC. The largest, built by King Khufu (or Cheops), is the only survivor of the original Seven Wonders of the World. It required roughly 2.3 million blocks of stone weighing an average of 2 1/2 tons each, with some weighing over 15 tons, heaped skywards from a base covering 13 acres (5.25 hectares). Rising to 480 ft (146 m), the stone mountain was the tallest building in the world for over four millennia, and it survives as an astonishing feat of engineering. It was a triumph of accurate calculation too, for in erecting this colossal piece of solid geometry the architects worked with minute precision, using set squares, plumb lines and rulers. The base of the pyramid is a near-perfect square, with right angles at the corners accurate to within one-twentieth of a degree. On top the builders fitted together some huge limestone blocks within one-fiftieth of an inch of each other.

Much forethought went into the construction. Before work could begin, the royal architects drew up designs, and astronomers laid out the north-south axis, so that the royal mummy in the tomb should be properly orientated towards the heavens. Surveyors used measuring cords to calculate distances, and it is thought that a level foundation was obtained by digging ditches and filling them with water whose flat surface served as a spirit level. Much of the limestone was quarried locally, by masons using copper chisels. The harder stone was split from the living rock with a row of wooden wedges, which were rammed into crevices, and then soaked with water so that they expanded to split the stone.

Granite slabs were needed particularly for the inner chambers, where they provided massive lintels that spread the colossal tonnage of masonry above the tombs. The granite had to be floated on barges 590 miles (950 km) down the Nile from Aswan. Draught animals were not used at this time, and given that the builders possessed no wheeled vehicles, pulleys, winches or cranes, getting the slabs to the site must have been a massive undertaking. The labourers hauled the heavy stone blocks on rollers and wooden sledges, using ropes of twisted papyrus. Then they raised them by means of mud-brick ramps which ran around the pyramid, lubricated with water, which were later dismantled. When building the inner core of the pyramid, some blocks were levered in flush with one another. Others were more roughly aligned and the spaces between them filled with a mortar of sand, clay and rubble. The core was afterwards encased in fine white limestone topped by a pyramidal block, or *pyramidion*. To face off the outer skin with perfect smoothness, the builders tested the sides with a cord that was pulled taut and treated with a red pigment that showed up any bumps.

The Greek historian Herodotus claimed that 100 000 slaves were used to build a pyramid. There is, however, no evidence that slaves were kept in any numbers under the Old Kingdom. Conscripts for the labouring gangs seem to have been drawn from the Egyptian villages much as they were for army service. And Herodotus greatly overestimated the size of the task force. Modern scholars estimate the work force for the Great Pyramid to have numbered some 4000-5000 men. They were organised in military-style units called *aperu* consisting of five groups of ten-man gangs. Each *aperu* had its own name: 'Khufu Calls for Love' was one of them. It has been estimated that as many as 250 men may have

been needed to haul the biggest of the granite blocks, weighing up to 40 tons. However, it is not necessary to picture these men as brutalised slave labourers.

WORKMAN'S PIETY
A labourer called
Nefersenut makes
an offering before
the goddess
Hathor.

PYRAMID OF KHAFRE

WORKERS' BARRACKS

BUILDING A PYRAMID

How the pyramids were built has long baffled Egyptologists. A number of different ideas have been suggested for the raising of the blocks – including a type of crane – but the most likely method involved the use of ramps. In recent years archaeologists have identified what they believe to be traces of these massive ramps. Much of the stone for the interior of the pyramid was quarried on site, and the ramps were constructed from the limestone chippings left from the working of the blocks, which were probably held together with mud and mud-brick. Gangs hauled the blocks on sleds and the way was eased with water. The pyramid was cased in fine limestone brought from quarries on the east bank of the Nile and while it was being finished, the ramps were demolished and the temples and causeway constructed. The capstone, or *pyramidion,* was often of granite with gilt inscriptions.

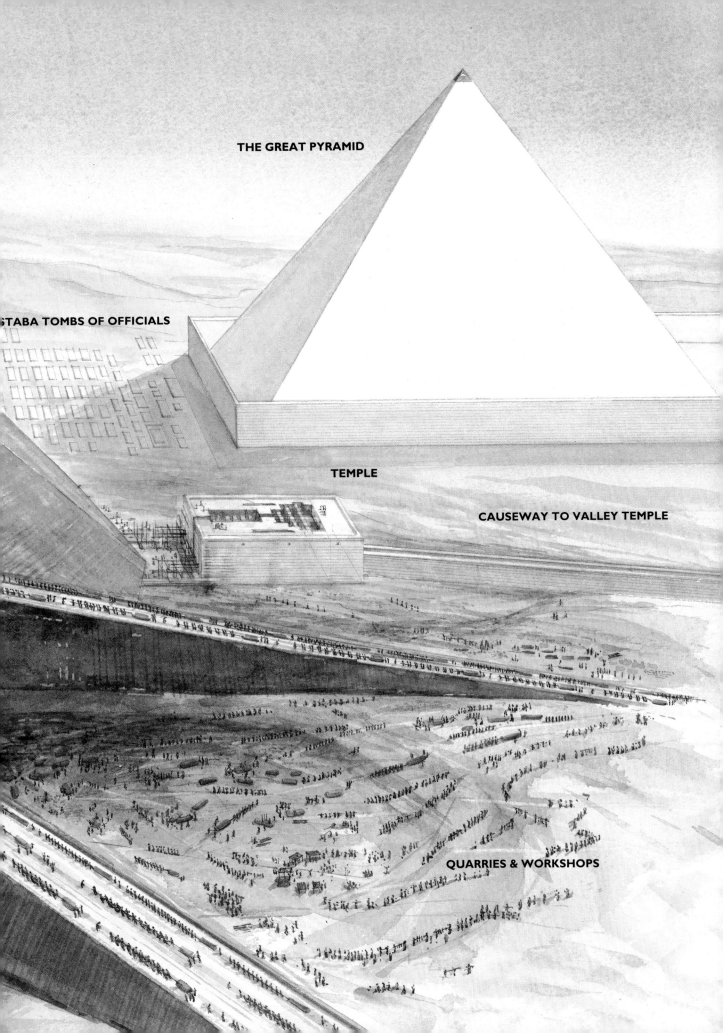

THE GREAT PYRAMID

MASTABA TOMBS OF OFFICIALS

TEMPLE

CAUSEWAY TO VALLEY TEMPLE

QUARRIES & WORKSHOPS

According to one foreman's report, the pyramid builders were so pleased to work for the pharaoh that they laboured without getting thirsty or exhausted and 'came home in good spirits, sated with bread, drunk with beer, as if it were the beautiful festival of a god'. This may well have been propaganda. But pyramid workers were certainly fed from the royal estates with daily measures of bread and beer, and a tomb inscription from the time of Mycerinus records that 'His Majesty desires that no one shall be compelled to the task, but that each should work to his own satisfaction'. The truth seems to be that the pyramid-builders were free citizens conscripted more or less willingly for a great national enterprise. The work may have been exhausting. But in helping to shape the pharaoh's immense machine for eternity all present approached the realm of the gods.

A 240 ft (73 m) long statue of the Great Sphinx guarded the pyramids. This mythological creature, with a lion's body and human head, was sculpted from an outcrop of rock by order of King Khafre, or Chephren (2558-2532 BC), who built the second of the pyramids, and it embodied all the wondrous majesty of Egypt's sovereign. Around each pyramid was a whole complex of buildings. At the Valley Building on the banks of the Nile, the pharaoh's body and the funeral offerings were brought ashore. The royal cortege arrived aboard funeral barges, and the barque bearing the king's coffin was hauled on a sledge along

TOMB CUTTER **Unshaven and overweight, a stonemason toils at the rock face.**

a causeway leading to the pyramid. In the Mortuary Temple at its terminus, the ceremony of the Opening of the Mouth was enacted; here, too, after burial, the priests continued to perform rituals every day so that the dead pharaoh's spirit should always be supplied with food and strength. The Egyptians at first believed that eternal life was granted only to the king, but courtiers and members of the royal family later started making provision for their own afterlives, with the result that subsidiary tombs grew up around the main pyramid complex, all paid for by the pharaoh as a mark of esteem for the favoured elite. All had to be supplied and tended by priests for generation after generation. Eventually the cost became ruinous for the royal treasury, and scholars cite the resulting depletion of national resources as a key reason for Egyptian decline at the end of the Old Kingdom.

IN THE VALLEY OF THE KINGS

By the Middle Kingdom period, religious beliefs had become more democratic and any Egyptian might, on principle, expect an afterlife. Royal pyramids were smaller, but the number of private burial chambers increased. In the New Kingdom settlement of Deir el-Medina on Luxor's west bank, tomb-workers toiling for the royal family received, along with a house and chattels, a tomb of their own. These were the men entrusted with cutting and furnishing the royal burial places in the Valley of the Kings, and they spent much of their spare time decorating their own tombs in the hills overlooking the village. The men were able to apply sophisticated skills to their own, humbler resting places. One of the finest surviving examples is the brightly coloured burial chamber of a workman called Sennejem, who lived in the south-western corner of the village next door to his father, Khabekhnet. On the wall facing the entrance to his tomb there is a superb painted figure of Osiris standing with crook and flail between two immense, brooding eyes. Inside, the dead man is seen

---

TIME OFF

Work for the tomb-makers in the Valley of the Kings was strenuous, but the men do not appear to have been exploited. Apart from regular holidays, they were granted leave of absence for all manner of personal reasons. Records show that these included family births, weddings and funerals, eye trouble, snakebite and even the need to take an ailing donkey to the vet.

worshipping the ancient gods, or toiling in the lush green fields of a magical hereafter.

Artisans like Sennejem divided their time between home life in the village and days spent on site in the Valley of the Kings, reached by a winding cliff path that snaked its way among the parched hills. Thutmose I first chose this remote spot as a burial place, on observing that just about every royal tomb in Egypt – including the pyramids – had been plundered by robbers. Subsequently, it became the practice for other pharaohs of the 18th, 19th and 20th dynasties to select the site for their Valley tomb soon after they came to the throne.

Once the location had been settled, the king called on the royal architect to draw up the ground plan. Then it was left to the stonemasons to cut their way into the rock face, a challenging task that might take them over 664 ft (200 m) into the bowels of the hills. They worked with porters behind to carry out the chippings in bags of leather or wicker. An ostracon, or fragment of broken pottery, now in the Cambridge Fitzwilliam Museum in Britain, shows a sketch of a stout-looking stonemason going about his business with chisel and mallet. He is bald and unshaven, and the effort of the work shows.

The walls were constructed with smooth surfaces, or plastered if necessary. Draughtsmen drew up a grid to transfer their designs to the walls, the figures being laid in first in broad washes of colour, and the details being added later. They

DEATHLESS GAZE Tutankhamun was buried in a series of mummy cases wrought from gilded wood, carved stone and solid gold.

HAULING A STATUE As the giant effigy is pulled on a sled, workmen lubricate the runners with water. Most of this type of heavy work was done during the flood season, using labourers taken from the flooded fields. The massive blocks and statues were almost completed in the quarries, so that faults in the stone were found before removal. Some abandoned, half-finished statues still lie in the desert quarries.

worked by the light of candles made from twisted canvas smeared with fat or oil, and to prevent smoke from damaging the reliefs, they applied salt to the candle wicks.

If a pharaoh died while work was still in progress, he risked burial in an unfinished tomb. Such was the case with the 18th-dynasty pharaoh Horemheb, who was laid to rest amid incomplete wall scenes, rubble and miscellaneous litter. But this was not typical. Altogether, 28 pharaohs were buried in the Valley of the Kings and their burials were generally accompanied by fantastic spectacles of wealth and grandeur. Evidence of great funerary

CONTAINERS The embalmed intestines of the dead were preserved in vessels known as canopic jars.

riches comes especially from the tomb of the boy king, Tutankhamun, which was located by archaeologist Howard Carter and Lord Carnarvon in 1922.

Though visited by robbers shortly after the pharaoh's death, Tutankhamun's inner tomb was virtually intact and crammed with furnishings and ornaments that display the supreme artistry of imperial Egypt. Here were gilded statues, chariots and couches, ebony gaming boards, painted caskets, ostrich fans and alabaster vases. Altogether, some 3000 objects would eventually be recovered from the tomb, which took nearly a decade to empty. The ultimate prize was the colossal quartzite sarcophagus, or coffin, of Tutankhamun himself, containing the mummy case of the dead pharaoh and its innermost coffin made from pure gold. Inside was the mummy, swathed in linen bandages in which the ancient priests had enfolded no fewer than 143 jewelled amulets to protect the pharaoh on his journey into the afterlife.

STANDING GUARD Tutankhamun's preserved organs were protected by a figure of the goddess Serket.

THE EGYPTIAN MIND

The brawn for monument-building was supplied by the great mass of the common people.

But the brains behind Egypt was the class of scribes whose profession incorporated everyone

from architect to dentist, from teacher to tax collector.

WHETHER CALCULATING the number of blocks needed for a pyramid, or the beer rations for a team of tomb-workers, the scribes were key figures in every enterprise. They were highly regarded professionals in ancient Egypt, for knowledge of reading and writing was essential to any official career, whether political, administrative, religious or military. In fact, members of the ruling class in ancient Egypt called themselves 'scribes' to distinguish themselves from the lower orders.

Elementary schooling began at about five years of age, and teachers did not believe in sparing the rod. In the words of the scribe Amenemope, 'The ear of the boy is on his backside. He listens when he is beaten.' Formal education seems to have been reserved for boys, and though some daughters of well-to-do families probably did learn to read and write there is no firm evidence of it. Women certainly composed letters, but these may well have been written for them by a male scribe in the household. Not a single document penned beyond doubt by a woman has survived from ancient Egypt. As women were barred from the state bureaucracy, it is likely that, in official eyes, they simply did not need to be literate.

Schoolboys lived at home and rushed off every morning to the school, or 'house of instruction', attached to a government building or temple. One document vividly evokes the age-old scramble from bed, as a father calls to his son, 'Awake! At your place! Your friends already have their books before them. Get your clothes, put your sandals right!' Lessons for the younger boys consisted of reciting sums and copying out standard texts. One basic primer, in use for over 1000 years, was the *Kemit* ('compendium') packed with model letters and useful phrases, as well as various wisdom texts containing

SCRIBE'S CHEST A container for writing materials dating from the New Kingdom period.

advice to aspiring scholars. Youngsters often began by writing on wooden tablets treated with a smooth white plaster that could be wiped clean for repeated use. Lessons went on all morning, and a lunch break at noon was probably followed by a siesta during the heat of the day. Schooling would have been resumed in the late afternoon.

Once the basics were mastered, would-be scribes could progress to more advanced learning, and the opportunity to write on papyrus. A body of texts now known as the *Miscellanies*, consisting of fragments of school texts, give some idea of the material that students had to master, such as lists of rare items, technical terms, hymns to particular gods and difficult mathematical problems. It seems that music formed part of the curriculum – perhaps in certain of the temple schools – for in one miscellany the teacher tells his pupil: 'You have been taught to sing to the reed pipe, to chant to the lute, to recite to the lyre.' Punishment for older pupils involved more than beatings. Miscreants might also be detained for days on end in the stocks, with wooden blocks, such as those normally used to hold criminals in prison, clamped around their feet.

In the *Miscellanies*, a favourite subject was the didactic treatise glorifying the scribe's

BRAIN WORK **The concentration shows in this small carved figure of a scribe, found at Amarna.**

MEDICINE MAN **King Zoser's Chief of Dentists and Physicians carries a scribe's tools over his shoulder.**

position in society and comparing it with the hardships of other crafts and professions. From this tradition came the *Satire on Trades,* which has given posterity many fascinating insights into the lives of Egypt's ordinary working people. The document's message is emphatic. No scribe ever goes short of food or of riches, so:

Spend the day writing with your fingers,
whilst reading by night.
Befriend the papyrus roll and the palette.
It pleases more than wine.

Officials expected their sons to succeed them in their jobs, and they had easy access to temple and palace schools. But it seems that the system also absorbed people from lower levels of society. Artisans such as draughtsmen and sculptors were often literate, and formed a privileged group in society. Nevertheless the majority of the population were illiterate.

THE 365-DAY YEAR

On completing their education, most scribes went straight into their chosen profession. But some would continue to study. In the temples, especially, priestly scribes spent much of their time poring over the papyrus rolls that contained their sacred texts. And

EGYPTIAN HIEROGLYPHS

The Egyptians devised a system of picture writing that has told the modern world much of what is known of their society.

CODE-BREAKING Two centuries of research have allowed scholars to decipher Egyptian hieroglyphs, one of the most decorative scripts ever devised.

A STARING EYE, a squatting man, a plumed reed, a slithering snake . . . laid out in row upon row, the symbols that comprise ancient Egyptian hieroglyphics baffled onlookers for generations. The Greeks called the script hieroglyphic ('sacred carving') in the belief that it had some occult religious meaning – as if the symbols formed part of some secret and mysterious rite. In reality, Egyptian hieroglyphics form a workmanlike system of writing which contains no special enigmas. The code was cracked following the discovery in 1799 of a black basalt slab, known as the Rosetta stone, during Napoleon's campaign in Egypt. This stone contained an inscription in three languages – hieroglyphic, demotic (a kind of shorthand hieroglyphic) and Greek – so that it proved possible to compare an Egyptian text with the same passage in a known language.

A young French scholar called Jean François Champollion was the first to gain some insight into the script. In 1822, he managed to identify the names of Cleopatra and Ptolemy in the Rosetta stone. The hieroglyphs, he found, conveyed meaning in a way that was partly pictorial and partly alphabetic. In its origin, this form of writing must have begun with simple pictures to stand for everyday objects, and developed so that some objects became more stylised.

Sometimes a hieroglyph simply represented what it resembled. The picture of a bee, for example,

Lord of the Two Lands Ra

Amun User-maet-mer (beloved-of) User-maet-re, beloved of Amun.

Lord of Appearances

Ra

mes

ses.

This column of text describes the action of the whole scene: 'Giving incense to his father Ptah'.

The signs in this column, as in the cartouches, are read from right to left and from top to bottom. The name of the god may be seen again in front of his face, but is there written from left to right.

The two cartouches enclose the king's birth name, Ra-mes-ses (Ramses), and his throne name, which was taken at the time of his accession. The name Ramses is flanked by two signs, the crook and the pillar, meaning 'Ruler of Heliopolis'.

PICTURE WRITING Hieroglyphs describe a king's presentation to the god Ptah, while the picture shows him offering incense from a censer like the one on the left.

represented a bee (or honey), and the picture of a man rejoicing stood for joy. But the system was refined so that a hieroglyph often represented a single consonant unrelated to the object depicted. So, for example, the plumed reed represented a 'y' sound, and the snake was a 'z'. Sometimes a hieroglyph stood for two or three sounds in combination: the beetle represented the sound 'kheper'. However, the Egyptians never bothered to insert vowels, so that reading hieroglyphics is like reading the English sentence 'handle with care' as 'hndl wth cr'.

By fitting together sound symbols, the Egyptian scribe could construct any sentence. The hieroglyph system was cumbersome, in the sense that the scribe had to draw a fairly detailed picture of an owl, for example, simply to obtain the letter 'm' and a quail chick for a 'w'. And the would-be scribe had to master a huge alphabet: some 700 symbols were in everyday use under the New Kingdom. Though hieroglyphics were reasonably well suited to the patient business of carving short inscriptions in stone, writing with reed pens on papyrus called for a faster, more flowing script. In response to this need, a simplified version known as 'hieratic' was devised. This was in use from the Old Kingdom up to the 8th century BC, and thereafter the even speedier and more stylised script known as demotic came into use.

DID YOU KNOW?

The 24-hour day was an invention of ancient Egypt, where scribes divided daylight and darkness into periods of 12 hours each. However, the lengths of daylight and darkness vary according to the season, so that the hours had to be elastic too. A daylight hour in midsummer was, for example, longer than one in winter. The Egyptians measured the hours with water clocks, and the instruments had to have different marks to indicate the hour at different times of year.

The 3000-year-old body of one mummified Egyptian girl has posed the experts a problem. The 13-year-old's flesh showed some evidence of decomposition, perhaps through immersion in water. Her skull and legs were broken – and her feet were missing. Scientists have surmised that she may have fallen prey to a crocodile.

the onset of the Nile floods, it made an appropriate beginning for the calendar year.

A 365-day calendar, devised by some unknown genius in the 3rd millennium BC, was one of the triumphs of Egyptian science. The Babylonians, who were more advanced astronomers, had developed a rather unsatisfactory calendar based on the cycles of the moon. In Egypt, too, for general purposes, the year was divided up into three seasons of four lunar months. But the 12 lunar months only amounted to 354 days, and Egypt's astronomers had noted that the solar year was just over 365 days. Since it was the sun's rays that quickened the crops and determined the pattern of the seasons, the Egyptian astronomers created a public solar calendar in which there were 12 months of 30 days, with five extra holidays at the end dedicated to the deities Osiris, Isis, Nephthys, Seth and Horus. (The true solar calendar contains an extra quarter of a day – the Egyptians had noticed this but it was only in Roman times that a 'leap year' system

scholarship took them into areas far outside the realm of theology. They studied astronomy, history, arithmetic, geometry, medicine and musical theory. Though supernatural beliefs permeated every aspect of their thought, the Egyptians also cradled the scientific spirit of experiment and analysis.

The astronomers on the flat roofs of temple buildings studied the heavens with keen interest. Since the prosperity of Egypt depended on correctly forecasting the seasons of flood and of sowing, the observation of recurring celestial events was vital. Egyptian astronomers identified five 'stars that know no rest' – the planets Mercury, Venus, Mars, Jupiter and Saturn. They also located many of the fixed stars, and calculated the time at night according to tables listing their movements over ten-day periods. Sirius – the brightest star – was of particular interest. New Year's Day in ancient Egypt fell on July 19 when Sirius reappeared on the eastern horizon just before sunrise, after a 70-day absence. As the event coincided with

SCHOOL DAYS **Much teaching in ancient Egypt was done in the open air.**

was adopted to cope with the discrepancy.)

In Egypt, each 30-day month was divided into three ten-day weeks, with days lasting 24 hours. To measure the hours, the Egyptians used a water clock, which worked on the principle of the hourglass: it consisted of a simple earthenware bowl, pierced at the bottom with several small holes through which the water escaped at a steady rate. The water level was read off against marks on the inside of the bowl to find out the time.

When making their calculations, the Egyptians used a decimal system of numbers deriving, it is thought, from the 10 fingers of the hand. When measuring, they employed the royal cubit, which was composed of seven hand widths – 20 $1/2$ in (52 cm) – as well as other measures based on the finger, forearm and so on. In general they approached problems practically rather than theoretically; for example, the scribes needed numbers chiefly to calculate crop yields for purposes of taxation, or such matters as the quantity of bricks needed to make a given building, of men needed to build it, and of corn to be rationed out per labourer. But although practical needs came first, various texts including a document known as the Rhind Mathematical Papyrus, written about 1600 BC, show that the Egyptians were also capable of more abstract calculations. They could handle fractions and solve equations involving unknown quantities.

The Egyptians were also familiar with elementary geometry. They could calculate the area of triangles and could find the area of a circle with reasonable accuracy. And some of the principles of solid geometry were known to them too: they could work out the volumes of a cylinder and a pyramid – particularly important for those working on the pharaohs' great tomb monuments at Giza.

A Charm Against Migraine

In medicine above all, the Egyptians excelled, and their physicians were famed throughout the ancient world. Clay tablets discovered at Amarna show that Egyptian doctors were often sent to foreign courts in Syria and Assyria. The

AILING MAN Image of a priest called Remi. His withered leg may have resulted from poliomyelitis.

kings of Persia employed Egyptian physicians, and the Greeks revered them as the fathers of medical science. Herodotus noted not only the number of doctors but the fact that they specialised in particular ailments: 'some in diseases of the eyes, others of the head, others of the teeth, others of the stomach and so on; while others, again, deal with the sorts of troubles which cannot be exactly localised.' Surviving medical texts indicate that Egyptian doctors had identified some 200 types of illness; their documents discuss everything from bone-setting to the treatment of hysteria, cystitis, ulcers and gonorrhoea. Though their terminology is sometimes obscure, it is often quite evident what condition they are discussing. So, for example, one document describes the state of a man with an open head wound. 'His mouth is locked tight,' runs the text, 'his brow is convulsively contorted and he has the expression of a man crying.' This is a diagnosis of tetanus, a disease caused by bacteria entering a wound and producing toxins that cause muscular spasms and rigidity in the jaw (hence the popular name, lockjaw).

It has often been said that Egyptian physicians gained detailed knowledge of human anatomy through the embalming practice of opening the abdomen and removing the internal organs. In reality, doctors took no part in the mummification process, which was the province of the priests of Anubis. Physicians learnt their

MEDICAL SPELL Carved basalt figure of a man displaying a magical text for healing.

SURGICAL INSTRUMENTS Egyptian physicians heated their knives and probes before application to wounds.

trade chiefly by studying ancient texts where the anatomy of animals was used for analogy more than that of humans. Butchers and cooks probably taught them more than embalmers, therefore.

The sophistication of Egyptian doctors should not be exaggerated, for there were formidable gaps and mistakes in their understanding of the body's workings. For example, doctors believed that the heart governed more than the flow of blood alone. They believed that it was the control centre of everything: the intelligence, the nerves and the tendons, the urine and the faeces. They imagined the heart to be connected to all parts of the body by channels known as *metu*, which, when blocked or polluted, caused illness, just as misfortune arose if something interfered with the normal flow of water through the Nile's canals. An Egyptian physician was also a magician, and the ancient texts were full of strange concoctions and ritual incantations to rid patients of evil spirits.

A TRIP TO THE DOCTOR

Despite all superstitions and misconceptions, however, Egyptian doctors did, by trial and error, achieve results. They learnt the use of many herbal remedies, prescribing castor oil, for example, as a laxative and powdered henbane and mandrake for their narcotic properties. In New Kingdom times opium was imported from Cyprus as a painkiller. Standards of hygiene were high because the Egyptians' obsession with ritual purity required surgeons and their assistants to wash themselves thoroughly before an operation. In addition, they heated all surgical blades and metal probes in the fire before use. Although this was done to help to staunch the flow of blood from incisions, it also lessened the risk of infection.

One of the most impressive features of Egyptian medicine was the doctors' systematic approach to diagnosis. A document known as the Edwin Smith Surgical Papyrus (named after its first owner following excavation) is considered a milestone in medical history for its level-headed investigation of physical injury. Here there is virtually no superstition. The treatise looks at 48 types of fracture, dislocation or wound, carefully describing the condition in each case. The text shows that a medical examination in Egypt was a very professional affair, with the doctor asking questions, smelling, feeling and probing with care. Patients were asked to walk or move their limbs to determine the area of injury. The doctor did not rush into a course of treatment. Rather than inflict unnecessary suffering on a patient, he would speak of 'an ailment not to be treated'. In uncertain cases he would refer to, 'an ailment with which I will contend'. Only if confident of a favourable outcome would he say, 'an ailment I will treat'.

Egyptian doctors knew the difference between the *sedj,* or simple fracture, and the *peshen* – a complicated fracture involving splintering of the bone. Broken bones were set with splints made of palm ribs, reeds or strips of bark bound with linen or plant fibre. Doctors employed sutures, clamps and adhesive plaster to seal wounds. They even engaged in the practice of trepanning – opening a patient's skull to relieve pressure on the brain. The operations appear to have worked, because mummies have been discovered with trepanned incisions that had healed long before the time of the person's death.

If a wealthy Egyptian's tooth fell out, he or she might have it fixed back into place with a 'bridge' of gold or silver wire attaching it to its sturdier neighbours; examples have been recovered from the mouths of several mummies. Egyptian dentists prescribed a mixture of resin and malachite (a mineral from which copper is obtained) for fillings. Opticians administered eye drops with a vulture's quill, and one ancient papyrus even discusses the different eye complaints suffered by animals. Veterinary medicine was important in Egypt, for many a farmer's prosperity depended on the health of his livestock. A treatment for a bull suffering from wind, or a cold, runs: 'Let him be laid on his side, let him be sprinkled with cold water, let his eyes and his hoofs and all his body be rubbed with gourds or melons, let him be fumigated with gourds.'

HEALTH OF THE NATION

Despite the very basic nature of the popular diet, the Egyptians appear to have been a healthy people. Bread and beer, eked out with occasional fruits, vegetables, fish and fowl, provided plain but wholesome fare. The poor were not prone to starve (except in rare times of national famine); and mummies show no evidence of widespread malnutrition. Among the elite, fed on red meat, wine and honeycakes, weight seems to have been the greater problem. Though tomb painters depict their patrons as young and slender, statues sometimes portray corpulent figures. And the study of mummies has revealed that over 10 per cent of them suffered from arteriosclerosis – a thickening of the arteries associated with fatty foods and a high-stress lifestyle.

Bumper food production certainly helped the population to expand at a steady rate from the time when Egypt was first united around 3000 BC. Estimates suggest that the first pharaoh governed a nation of some 870 000 people. The population had grown to 1.6 million by 2500 BC, around the time when the Great Pyramid was built. For the height of the New Kingdom around 1250 BC, a figure of 4 million people is often quoted.

X-rays and CAT scans of mummies have revealed a multitude of disorders in the Egyptians, from impacted wisdom teeth to poliomyelitis. A 19th-dynasty king called Siptah had a deformed foot, which was shown by X-ray analysis to have the bone damage and atrophied muscles characteristic of polio. This infectious complaint seems to have been quite common. An 18th-dynasty priest named Remi is depicted on a tomb carving with a similarly withered leg, and a foot stretching to the ground to compensate.

Spinal tuberculosis, a bacterial disease causing hunched backs and other angular deformations, has been identified in a number of bodies. Among the remains of working people, scientists have also found evidence of spinal osteophytosis. This is a disorder of the spine characterised by small outgrowths of bone on the vertebrae. It can result from overworking the back in just such a way as hauling grain sacks, loading bricks or carrying water jars. Among the bodies of ordinary people, just about everyone in the 40-50 age group shows some evidence of it. Among the mummified bodies found in tombs of the elite it is much less common – clear evidence that the land of the pharaohs was always a land of two nations existing side by side.

BACK-BREAKING TOIL
Bodies of working people often exhibit signs of spinal disorder.

TIME CHART

POLITICAL HISTORY OF EGYPT

EARLY DYNASTIC
3150-2686 BC

3150-3050 BC Upper and Lower Egypt are united under the first pharaohs, 'Scorpion' and Narmer (or 'Menes'). The city of Memphis is founded.

3050-2890 BC 1st dynasty. Pharaohs are: Aha, Djer, Djet, Den, Andjib, Semerkhet, Qaa.

2890-2686 BC 2nd dynasty. Pharaohs are: Hetepsekhemwy, Raneb, Ninetjer, Peribsen, Khasekhem.

OLD KINGDOM 2686-2181 BC

2686-2613 BC 3rd dynasty. In the reign of Djoser, the Step Pyramid is built at Saqqara, designed by Djoser's minister and architect, Imhotep. Pharaohs are: Sanakhte, Neterykhet (Djoser), Sekhemkhet, Huni.

2613-2498 BC 4th dynasty. The age of pyramids reaches its peak with buildings at Giza by Khufu (Cheops) and his successors. Pharaohs begin penetration of Nubia and Sinai to protect Egypt's frontiers and guarantee supplies of valuable raw materials. Pharaohs are: Sneferu, Khufu (Cheops),

NARMER One of the first pharaohs of united Egypt.

Radjedef, Khaefre (Chephren), Menkaure (Mycerinus), Shepseskaf.

2498-2345 BC 5th dynasty. Cult of sun god Re becomes predominant in Egypt. Pharaohs are: Userkaf, Sahure, Neferirkare, Shepseskare, Raneferef, Neuserre, Menkauhor, Djedkare, Unas.

2345-2181 BC 6th dynasty. Power of pharaohs passes more into hands of provincial nobility; this heralds a period of disunity. Pharaohs are: Teti, Pepy I, Merenre I, Pepy II, Merenre II. Queen Nitiqert.

**KING USERKAF
A Pharaoh of the 5th dynasty.**

CHRONOLOGY OF EVERYDAY LIFE

MAIN ARTERY The Nile was Egypt's thorough-fare, and boats of wood and reed were used from earliest times.

c.3000 BC Hieroglyphic writing and papyrus are already in use in Egypt. A decimal system is employed for calculation. Both sexes wear eye make-up and men shave with stone razors. The Egyptians sail the Nile in reed boats. The first pharaohs are buried in large tombs at Abydos, surrounded by the graves of their retainers, dwarf attendants and pet dogs.

c.2800 BC The 365-day year and 24-hour day are in use. Egyptians start to employ copper tools. Pottery is cast on a turntable wheel. Egyptian stoneware is exported to Syria.

c.2670 BC King Djoser builds Step Pyramid at Saqqara. Heliopolis comes to prominence as cult centre of the sun god Re. Royal shipyards are founded, where sizable wooden vessels are built. On noblemen's estates, measuring tubs for calculating taxes in corn are in use.

c.2600 BC The great pyramids and Sphinx are built at Giza, following the pyramids at Dashur and Meidum.

c.2500 BC Egyptian farmers start to employ the plough. Circular mirrors of polished copper come into use.

2350 BC The first 'Pyramid Texts' – spells designed to help the pharaoh through the afterlife – are carved on walls of the tomb of Unas.

CALCULATING THE YIELD Grain was measured and stored to safeguard against years of famine.

THE REST OF THE WORLD

3000 BC Mesopotamia: Sumerian city-states are already flourishing; cuneiform writing, bronze technology, the wheel and the plough are in use. Soap is made by boiling alkalis. Mesopotamia is united under Sargon of Akkad (2371-2316).

3000 BC Crete: beginning of Minoan civilisation.

2750 BC Britain: Stonehenge monument is begun in England.

2700 BC Bible lands: Egyptians trade with Byblos in Lebanon.

2400 BC India: beginning of Indus Valley civilisation.

STANDARD TRANSPORT In this Sumerian standard from Ur, the chariots are drawn by asses.

2181–1797 BC

2181-2160 BC 7th-8th dynasties. Long period of strife opens between provincial officials contesting the different nomes (or regions) into which Egypt is divided. Famine and poverty are widespread. Libyans and Bedouins infiltrate pastures of the Delta. King lists refer to many pharaohs during this period, none ruling for more than a year or two.

FIRST INTERMEDIATE PERIOD

2160-2130 BC 9th dynasty.

2130-2033 BC 10th dynasty.

2133-2033 BC 11th dynasty. Period of powerful local rulers, the most important at Herakleopolis near the Faiyum, and at Thebes in the south. Conflict between different regions.

MIDDLE KINGDOM

2033-1973 BC 11th dynasty. Theban ruler, Mentuhótep II, reunites Egypt and begins period of consolidation. He founds a new capital at Itjet-tawy, south of Memphis.

1973-1797 BC 12th dynasty. Era of outstanding artistic

REFUGEES Libyans were forced into Egypt by famine.

achievement in Egypt, especially under Senusret III and Amenemhat III. Military expansion into Nubia and fortresses built there to protect trade routes. Pharaohs are: Amenemhat I, Senusret I, Amenemhat II, Senusret II, Senusret III, Amenemhat III, Amenemhat IV, Queen Sebekneferu.

SENUSRET III He was the pharaoh who expanded Egyptian control into Nubia.

c.2190-2106 BC Amid unrest of 1st intermediate period, increasing numbers of minor lords prepare opulent tombs for themselves; a lavish burial ceases to be the prerogative of kings. The famine and civil disorder of the age are later recalled by scribes in pessimistic works such as the *Admonitions of Ipuwer* and a discourse on the duties of kingship called *Teaching for Merikare*.

c.2106 BC Cult of Osiris rapidly spreads from his

LIFE AFTER DEATH The god Osiris became the means of an afterlife for all Egyptians.

centre of worship at Abydos.

c.2000 BC As a result of contact with Syria, bronze comes into widespread use.

1963-1786 BC 12th Dynasty is marked by flourishing of the arts. Literary classics of the time

POKING FUN Egyptian art often displays a sense of humour, as in this picture which satirises the funerary art of the ruling class.

include the *Story of Sinuhe* and the *Satire on Trades*. Tomb paintings of the period offer many vivid glimpses of daily life on nobles' estates. Egyptians import quantities of pottery from Crete.

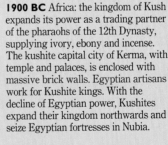

2100 BC Mesopotamia: first ziggurat, or step pyramid, is built at Ur. Hammurabi founds Babylonian Empire (1792 BC) and formulates law code. Mathematics and medicine flourish.

2000 BC Bible lands: Canaan is settled by Hebrews under Abraham.

2000 BC Europe: Carnac megaliths set up in France. Aryans enter Europe. Mycenaeans invade southern Greece (1900 BC).

2000 BC Crete: Linear A writing is developed.

2000 BC India: Aryan invasions begin.

1900 BC Africa: the kingdom of Kush expands its power as a trading partner of the pharaohs of the 12th Dynasty, supplying ivory, ebony and incense. The kushite capital city of Kerma, with temple and palaces, is enclosed with massive brick walls. Egyptian artisans work for Kushite kings. With the decline of Egyptian power, Kushites expand their kingdom northwards and seize Egyptian fortresses in Nubia.

LAW GIVER Hammurabi of Babylon codified the laws. Other tablets from Sumeria detail economic life.

1796–1540 BC

KING AHMOSE'S AXE Beneath an image of the king smiting his enemies, the war god, Monthu, is shown as a griffin. This unusual motif might show foreign influence.

1796-1660 BC 13th dynasty. Egypt begins to lose control of Nubia.

SECOND INTERMEDIATE PERIOD

1660-1555 BC 15th dynasty. Asiatics known as the 'Hyksos' settle in increasing numbers in Egypt, and their rulers gradually extend their control over the Delta and Middle Egypt. The kings adopt the style of Egyptian pharaohs and rule from their Delta stronghold at Avaris.

1660-1570 BC 17th dynasty (ruling at Thebes). A separate Upper Egyptian principality comes into being under the princes of Thebes. Conflict breaks out between the Theban and Hyksos pharaohs. Nubia is under the control of the kings of Kush.

BEATING THE BOUNDS Chariots were prestige items of the nobility. In this representation of officials checking the boundaries of the temple fields, one is drawn by horses, which had to be imported from Syria, and the other by mules.

c.1786-1540 BC The horse-drawn chariot is adopted in Egypt, under the influence of Hyksos invaders, with horses imported from northern Syria. The Hyksos also bring an upright loom for improved weaving, and new musical instruments: the lyre, long-necked lute, oboe and tambourine. The hump-backed bull, olive and pomegranate tree appear in Egypt. In burial customs, the box-like coffin of earlier times is replaced by a humanoid case decorated to represent the deceased.

c.1660 BC The Rhind Mathematical Papyrus, dating from this time, demonstrates Egyptian knowledge of fractions and equations.

DEATH MASK The gold 'Mask of Agamemnon' was found in the royal tombs at Mycenae. Trade contacts between Egypt and the Aegean began during the Middle Kingdom and spread to include Mycenae in the 18th dynasty.

c.1550 BC In excavations at the site of the Hyksos capital of Avaris in the Nile's eastern Delta, archaeologists have found fragments of Minoan wall paintings showing the bull-leaping ceremony. The Hyksos had strong trade contacts with Asia, as well as the Aegean and Kush. As a result of these contacts, foreign styles had some influence on Egyptian artists during the New Kingdom.

representing simple objects and activities. Shang dynasty is founded (1600 BC) in the valley of the Yellow River.

1600 BC Bible lands: Hebrews migrate to Egypt.

1700 BC Africa: Kushite kingdom expands and absorbs former Egyptian territories of Nubia and trades directly with Hyksos rulers in the north of Egypt. The last rulers are buried in massive tumuli with sacrificed servants.

1740 BC Mesopotamia: horses and war chariots are introduced from Persia.

1650 BC Crete: Linear B writing (an early form of Greek) comes into use. Great palaces are built at Knossos and Phaistos.

1650 BC Greece: Mycenaean civilisation begins. First swords are found in Mycenaean graves.

1700 BC China: first written characters in Chinese appear,

WORLD ART A school of dolphins from a Minoan fresco in the royal palace at Knossos in Crete. Left: Shang dynasty bronze vessel.

1570–1070 BC

New Kingdom

1570-1293 BC 18th dynasty. Theban ruler, Ahmose, expels Hyksos from the Delta and regains control of part of Nubia. A golden age of Egyptian history dawns, with unparalleled prosperity and empire-building exploits in Syria, Nubia and Kush. Cult of Amun-Re predominates in Egypt. Female pharaoh, Hatshepsut, opens direct communications with the Land

of Punt. Thutmose III extends Egypt's frontiers. Great building works at Karnak and Luxor. 'Heretic' king Akhenaten establishes new royal city at Amarna, but orthodoxy returns under Tutankhamun. Horemheb restores Egypt's internal stability, permitting further campaigns in western Asia. Pharaohs are: Ahmose, Amenhotep I-III, Thutmose I-IV, Hatshepsut, Akhenaten, Smenkhkare, Tutankhamun, Ay, Horemheb.

Forced Labour Kushite prisoners of war were employed in the army, the palace and on temple estates. Other Kushites held high offices at court.

1293-1185 BC 19th dynasty. Ramses II sponsors gigantic building works, including monumental rock-cut temple complex at Abu Simbel. Major clashes with Hittites result in treaty defining 'spheres of interest' in Syria. Pharaohs are: Ramesses I-II, Sety I-II, Merneptah, Siptah, Queen Tawosret.

1185-1070 BC 20th dynasty. Combined forces of Libyans and so-called 'Sea Peoples' from western Asia are repulsed on land and sea by Ramses III. The Egyptian Empire in western Asia is lost in the reign of Ramses VI and control of Nubia by Ramses XI. Robbery of royal tombs. Pharaohs are: Sethnakhte, Ramses III- XI.

c.1550 BC Golden Age of Egyptian civilisation opens with the New Kingdom dynasties. Professional soldiers (as distinct from conscripted peasants) are employed in the imperial armies. Products of Nubia and Kush flood into Egypt: gold, ebony, ivory, cattle, gums, resins and semiprecious stones. A taste for colour and ornament runs riot in fashion and the arts. An erotic element enters painting, and love poetry exhibits genuine charm and emotion. Temples are built on an enormous scale and decorated with colossal statuary.

c.1353-1335 BC Reign of Akhenaten marks cultural revolution in Egypt, known as the 'Amarna period'. Painters abandon rigid formulae for a new naturalism. Akhenaten's Hymn to the Aten displays Egyptian lyric poetry at its height.

c.1295 BC The *shaduf,* a bucket-and-pole device, improves irrigation in Egypt. Metalworking is revolutionised

Mercenaries Professional soldiers, many of them mercenaries, policed Egypt's empire. Of these, the Libyans rose to the greatest power.

as bellows replace the blowpipe.

c.1100 BC World's oldest known map is drawn up, showing gold mines of Wadi Hammamat..

1500 BC Asia: Hittites develop iron technology. Ancient city of Troy, near the Dardanelles, is destroyed (traditional date, 1184 BC).

1450 BC Africa: the Kushite kingdom is brought to an end by the military campaigns of the Egyptian pharaohs. Nubia becomes a province of Egypt under the rule of a Viceroy, but local vassal rulers retain some power.

1400 BC Crete: Minoan civilisation falls; Mycenaeans take over (1350 BC).

1300 BC Central America: Olmecs in Mexico found first great civilisation in the Americas.

1200 BC Bible lands: Hebrews settle Israel. Alphabetic script is in use in Byblos and Ugarit.

Mighty Assyrians The Assyrian war machine, depicted here in the bronze gates of Balawat, expanded the Empire's power over western Asia.

1115 BC Mesopotamia: Assyrian Empire is established, with the accession of Tiglath-pileser I.

1100 BC China: Zhou dynasty extends Chinese civilisation and presides over foundation of traditional feudal society.

1070–656 BC

THIRD INTERMEDIATE PERIOD

1070-945 BC 21st dynasty. Egypt is ruled by a dynasty of pharaohs at Tanis in the Delta whose relatives were high priests of Amun at Thebes. Pharaohs are: Nesubanebdjed (Smendes), Psibkhanno (Psusennes I), Amenemope, Siamun.

945-700 BC 22nd and 23rd dynasties. Libyan kings. After the reign of Osorkon II there is a number of kingdoms throughout the country. Around 740 BC the Kushite king Kashta seizes control of Upper Egypt. Pharaohs are: Shoshenq I-V, Osorkon

I- III, Takeloth I-III, Pimay, Pedubast, Nimlot, Peftjauawybast.

716-710 BC 24th dynasty. Tefnakht, the Libyan prince of Sais in the western Delta, expands his kingdom to Memphis but is defeated by the Kushite king Piye (c.730 BC). Tefnakht's successor, Bakenranef, assumes the kingship.

710-656 BC 25th dynasty. The Kushite (Nubian) pharaoh Shabaqo defeats Bakenranef and becomes ruler of all Egypt. Assyrians invade Egypt (671 BC). Pharaohs are: Shabaqo, Shebitqo, Taharqo, Tanwetamani.

BRONZE-WORKING As these images of the pharaoh Pimay and the cat goddess Bastet (left) show, bronze work was one of the finest achievements of the Libyan period.

945 BC With the rise of the cult centre at Bubastis, worship of the cat goddess Bastet becomes widespread. General increase in the worship of gods incarnate as animals.

c.950 BC Changes in funerary practices, notably in the Theban region. The mummy is now enclosed in a case of cartonnage (linen and plaster), which was elaborately painted, then placed inside the wooden coffins. Instead of painted tombs, mummies are buried in pits or re-used tombs, often as family groups. Furniture, wooden models and household objects were no longer buried with the dead, but ushabti

figures, funerary papyri and figures of the god Osiris are placed in the graves. Large tombs are built again from around 700 BC.

c.700 BC During the later Libyan, Kushite and Saite periods there is a deep interest in Egypt's past, affecting art, religion and literature and leading to a period of great artistic achievement.

c.700 BC Demotic script comes into use, employing symbols so simplified that hieroglyphic picture-images are unrecognisable.

IVORY WORKING Ivory was one of the great Phoenician and Syrian crafts of the 9th-8th centuries BC. It was probably traded from Kush through Egypt or along the Red Sea.

1000 BC Mesopotamia: iron comes into use. Babylonian astronomers predict eclipses (c.750 BC). Assyrians destroy Babylon (689 BC).

1000 BC Africa: kingdom of Kush (the Sudan) re-emerges as a major power; royal tombs and pyramids are built (800 BC). About 750 BC the Kushite kings conquer southern Egypt. From 711 they rule the whole country, and establish an empire stretching from the Mediterranean far into Africa.

900 BC Europe: iron comes into common use.

814 BC Africa: Phoenicians sail along north African coast founding colonies, including Carthage. They establish

trading centres in Spain and exploit silver mines at Rio Tinto.

800 BC Greece: Greek alphabet is developed. Epic poetry of Homer is said to date from this time. First Olympic Games are held at Olympia (776 BC).

800 BC India: Hindu caste system develops.

800 BC Italy: Etruscans found fortress towns. Romulus is said to have founded Rome, 753 BC. Phoenicians trading in south Italy and Sicily.

ETRUSCAN EXPORTS A loving couple from the lid of an Etruscan sarcophagus. The sophisticated Etruscan civilisation of Italy traded with the Phoenicians, who brought objects from Egypt and the Aegean world.

664–332 BC

POLITICAL HISTORY OF EGYPT

LATE PERIOD

664-525 BC 26th dynasty. The princes of Sais, with Assyrian support, eventually reunite Egypt. Greek merchants develop settlements in Lower Egypt. A period of high artistic achievement and interest in the past. Revival is checked in 525 BC with Persian invasion. Pharaohs are: Nekau I-II, Psamtik I-III, Haaibre (Apries), Ahmose (Amosis).

525-404 BC 27th dynasty. Egypt becomes a province of the Persian Empire. Persians codify laws, initiate new building programmes and restore efficient administration.

404-343 BC 28th-30th dynasties. Last period of rule by native dynasties. Pharaohs are: Amyrteos, Nefaurud I, Pshenmut, Hakor, Nefaurud II, Nekhtnebef (Nectanebo I), Djeho (Teos), Nekhthorheb (Nectanebo II).

343-332 BC Second period of Persian rule, ending in 332 BC when the Macedonian king, Alexander the Great, wins Egypt. Thereafter the country falls under Greek rule, with the dynasty founded by Alexander's general Ptolemy, until the Romans defeat the last of the family, Cleopatra VII. Egypt becomes part of the Roman empire (30 BC).

HEAD MAN The reign of Nekhtnebef was Egypt's last long period of peace under a native king.

---

c.550 BC Iron-smelting begins at Greek trading centre of Naucratis in the western Delta. Other foreign trading quarters in the city of Memphis. World's first-known pin-tumbler lock is made.

664-525 BC 26th dynasty is marked by a return to traditional values in the arts, scholarship and administration.

c.525 BC Revival of Egyptian orthodoxy is interrupted by Persian invasion. Under Persian rule, government business is conducted in Aramaic (the language of the Persian

ELECTRUM COIN This coin from Ephesus is the earliest to have writing on it.

Empire), and some officials adopt Persian dress. Jewish colony at Elephantine (Aswan), with their own temple.

c.450 BC Greek historian, Herodotus,

ANIMAL EXPORT Baboons were brought from the interior of Africa from the earliest times. They were kept as pets by the nobility and sent to western Asia and Italy, along with other exotic animals, until Roman times.

visits Egypt and writes first full account of the country to have survived.

c.332 BC Following conquest by Alexander, Greek colonists flock to Egypt. Introduction of waterwheel revolutionises irrigation. Ptolemaic kings reside in Alexandria and the Egyptian peasant population has few rights.

CHRONOLOGY OF EVERYDAY LIFE

650 BC Asia Minor: coinage comes into use in kingdom of Lydia; it is made of electrum (a gold and silver alloy).

600 BC Italy: Romans devise their own alphabet. First pulley is attributed to Archytas of Tarentum (400 BC). Gauls sack Rome (390 BC).

551 BC China: Confucius is born. Lao-tse founds Taoism (c.550 BC). Carpets are in use. Chinese play a version of football (500 BC).

546 BC Persia: Cyrus the Great founds empire; widespread conquests follow.

530 BC India: Buddha begins teaching.

500 BC Africa: Nok civilisation flourishes in Nigeria. Hanno of Carthage explores coast of West Africa

(c.480 BC). Kushite kingdom continues, ruling from Meroe (Sudan).

490 BC Greece: Persians are repelled at Marathon. Athenian 'golden age' dawns with beginning of classic sculpture and temple-building. Oldest surviving Greek play is *The Persians* (472 BC) by Aeschylus. Socrates begins teaching (c.421 BC). Sparta defeats Athens at conclusion of Peloponnesian War (404 BC).

334 BC Macedonia: Alexander the Great begins conquest of the Persian empire. He defeats King Darius (333 BC), reduces Tyre and proceeds with conquests of Egypt and Babylon.

GREEK WARRIOR Alexander the Great of Macedon.

THE REST OF THE WORLD

INDEX

Acknowledgments

Abbreviations: T = Top; M = Middle; B = Bottom; R = Right; L = Left.
AKG, Berlin = Archiv für Kunst und Geschicte; BPK, Berlin = Bildarchiv Preussischer Kulturbesitz

1 *Funerary Model*, 11th Dynasty, Egyptian Museum, Berlin (Bodemuseum)/ BPK, Berlin/ Photography Jürgen Liepe. **2-3** *Relief from Tomb of Akhhetep*, 5th Dynasty, Louvre, Paris/ Giraudon. **4** *Priest Teuti and his wife*, 5th Dynasty, Egyptian Museum, Berlin,(ÄM 12547)(Charlottenburg)/ BPK, Berlin/ Photography M.Büsing, TL; *Wall Painting from Tomb of Panehesy, Thebes*, TR; *Scribe and Monkey-God Thoth*, 18th Dynasty, Louvre, Paris/ The Bridgeman Art Library, London, M; *Wall Painting from Tomb of Horemheb, Thebes*, 18th Dynasty, B. **5** *Cosmetic Spoon from Medinet Gurob*, 18th Dynasty, Egyptian Museum, Berlin, (ÄM 17337) (Bodemuseum)/ BPK, Berlin/ Photography Jürgen Liepe, TL; *Wall Painting from the Tomb of Ramose*, 18th Dynasty / AGK, Berlin/ Photography by Eric Lessing, TR; *Wall Painting from Tomb of Sennedjem Deir el-medina*, 19th Dynasty / AGK, Berlin/ Photography Eric Lessing, M; *Sphinx from temple of Hatshepsut, Thebes, Deir el Bahari*, 18th Dynasty, Egyptian Museum, Berlin (Bodemuseum)/ BPK, Berlin/ Photography Jürgen Liepe, B. **6-7** Illustration by Michael Shoebridge. **8** *Decorative Tiles from Thebes, Medinet Habu, Palace of Ramesses III*, 20th Dynasty, Egyptian Museum, Cairo/ Photography Jürgen Liepe. **9** *Painted Relief*, 5th Dynasty, Egyptian Museum, Berlin, (ÄM 2170)(Charlottenburg)/ BPK, Berlin/ Photography M. Büsing. **10** *Detail from Narmer's Palette from Hierakonpolis (Kom el Ahmar)*, Dynasty 0, Egyptian Museum, Cairo, (CG 14716)/ Giraudon. **11** *Funerary Model*, 12th Dynasty, Egyptian Museum, Berlin, (VÄGM 10-80) (Charlottenburg)/ Bildarchiv Preussischer Kulterbesitz/ Photography M. Büsing. **12** *Statue of Antinous*, 130-138 AD, Vatican Museum, Rome/ Scala, L; *The Banquet of Cleopatra, oil painting by Tiepolo*, National Gallery, London, R. **13** *Prussian Expedition to Pyramid of Cheops, Giza, colour lithograph by J.J.Frey*, 1842, Egyptian Museum, Berlin (Charlottenburg)/ BPK, Berlin/ Photography M. Büsing, T; *Bust of Richard Lepsius, Tomb of Mariette*, Egyptian Museum, Cairo/ Robert Morkot, M; *Howard Carter at Theban Excavations*, 1913 / Highclere Castle (Carnarvon Archive), BL; *Antechamber of Tutankhamun's Tomb, 1922* / Times Newspapers/ C.N. Reeves, BR. **14** *Wooden Shabti box of Priestess Hemtmehyt*, 19th to 20th Dynasty, British Museum, London. **15** *Funerary Model from Tomb of Meketre, Thebes*, 11th Dynasty, Egyptian Museum, Cairo, (JE 46715)/ Photography Jürgen Liepe. **16** *Wall Painting from Tomb of Nakht*, 18th Dynasty / Photography Dr. Abdel-Ghaffar Shedid. **17** *Akhenaten with his wife Nefertiti and their children, relief from Amarna*, 18th Dynasty, Egyptian Museum, Berlin, (ÄM 14145) (Charlottenburg)/ BPK, Berlin/ Photography M. Büsing. **18** *Wooden Statue*, Old Kingdom, Louvre, Paris/ Lauros-Giraudon. **19** *Wall Painting from Tomb of Anherkhau, Deir el-Medina, Thebes*, 20th Dynasty / AGK, Berlin/ Photography Eric Lessing, TL; *Marriage Contract, papyrus*, 172 BC, British Museum, London, (no: 10593), MR; *Gold Throne from Tomb of Tutankhamun, Thebes, Valley of the Kings*, Egyptian Museum, Cairo, (JE 62028)/ Robert Harding Picture Library, BL. **20** Illustration by Gill Tomblin. **21** *Wooden Statue of the Lady Tuya*, 18th Dynasty, Louvre, Paris/ Lauros-Giraudon, R; *Scene from Satirical Papyrus*, British Museum, London, (no: 10016) / E.T. Archive, L. **22** *Painted Relief of Sety I and Hathor from Tomb of Sety I, Valley of the Kings, Thebes*, 19th Dynasty, Museo Archeologico, Florence/ Scala. **23** *Painting from Tomb of Anherkhau, Deir el-Medina, Thebes*, 20th Dynasty / Werner Forman Archive/ Photography Dr. E. Strouhal. **24** *Colossus of Ramesses II from Temple of Amun, Karnak*/ A.A.M. Van der Heyden, Amsterdam, T; *Funerary Papyrus of Lady Cheritwebeschet*, 21st Dynasty, Egyptian Museum, Cairo/ Werner Forman Archive, B. **25** *Votive Stela from Deir el-Medina*, 19th Dynasty, Kingston Lacy, Bankes Collection (Stela no.7)/ National Trust, T; *Servant Girl, Wooden Statue*, Oriental Museum, Durham University/ The Bridgeman Art Library, M; *Funerary Model*, Middle Kingdom / Ashmolean Museum, Oxford, (no. 1921 . 1423), B. **26** *Painting of Akhenaten and Nefertiti, from Amarna*, 18th Dynasty, Egyptian Museum, Berlin, (ÄM 15000) (Charlottenburg) BPK, Berlin/ Photography M. Büsing, T. **27** *Statuette of Concubine*, 18th Dynasty, Brooklyn Museum, New York/ Werner Forman Archive, L; *Painted limestone statues of Rahotep and wife*, 4th Dynasty, Meidum, Egyptian Museum, Cairo, (no. C.G. 3 + CG4)/ Werner Forman Archive, B. **28** Illustration by Gill Tomblin, T; *Detail of an inscription*, Graeco-Roman Period, British Museum, London, (no: 1062), B. **29** *Relief from Temple of Hathor at Dendera*, Ptolemaic, Egyptian Museum, Cairo/ Werner Forman Archive. **30** *Wall Painting from Tomb of Menna, Thebes*, 18th Dynasty, L; *Wooden Statuette of Bes*, 19th Dynasty, British Museum, London/ Werner Forman Archive, M; *Wooden amulet*, 19th Dynasty, British Museum, London/Werner Forman Archive, R. **31** *Statue from Tomb of Seneb, Giza*, 4th Dynasty, Egyptian Museum, Cairo (JE 51280)/ Giraudon **32** *Jar*, 18th Dynasty, Egyptian Museum, Berlin, (ÄM 14476)/ BPK, Berlin/ Photography Jürgen Liepe, L; *Ebony Statuette*, Egyptian Museum, Berlin, (Bodemuseum)/ Werner Forman Archive, R. **33** *Wall Painting from Amarna*, 18th Dynasty, Ashmolean Museum, Oxford/ Artephot/ Photography M. Babey. **34** *Wall Painting from Tomb of Amen-Hi-r-khepeshef, Valley of the Queens, Thebes*, 20th Dynasty / Werner Forman Archive/ Photography Dr. E. Strouhal. **35** *Nubians from Tomb of Huy*, 18th Dynasty/ Werner Forman Archive/ Photograhy Dr. E. Strouhal. **36** *Statue of Isis*, Louvre, Paris/ Artephot/ Held. **37** *Wall Painting from Tomb of Nebamun, Thebes*/ The Bridgeman Art Library, T; *Wall Painting from Tomb of Sennedjem, Deir el-Medina, Thebes*, 19th Dynasty, B. **38** *Pleated Dress*, 1st Dynasty, Tarkham, University College, London, Petrie Museum, T; *Draught Board*, 19th-20th Dynasty,British Museum, London/ The Bridgeman Art Library, BL; *Wooden Horse from Akhmim*, British Museum, London/ Michael Holford, BR. **39** *Relief from Tomb of Mereruka Saqqara*, 6th Dynasty/ Werner Forman Archive, T; Painted *Limestone Statuette from Tomb of Ny-kau-inpu, Giza*, 5th-6th Dynasty, Oriental Institute of University of Chicago, B. **40-41** Illustrations by Gill Tomblin. **41** *Limestone Ostracon from Deir el-Medina*, New Kingdom / Medelhavsmuseet, Stockholm, (MM 14116), TR. **42** *Bronze Cat*, Late Period, Egyptian Museum, Berlin, (ÄM 11385)/ BPK, Berlin/ Photography M. Büsing. **43** *Wall Painting from Tomb of Menna, Thebes*, 18th Dynasty,TR; *Mummified Cat*, Late Period, Louvre, Paris/ The Bridgeman Art Library, BL. **44** *Wall Painting from Tomb of Menna, Thebes*, 18th Dynasty/ Werner Forman Archive, T; *Wooden Statue of Young Adult from Tomb at Sedment*, 6th Dynasty, NY Carlsberg Glptotek, Copenhagen, B. **45** *Painted Relief, Thebes, Asasif*, 11th Dynasty, Egyptian Museum Cairo/ Photography Jürgen Liepe. **46** *Limestone Model*, New Kingdom, Louvre, Paris/ The Bridgeman Art Library, L; *Papyrus depicting house of Nakht*, 18th Dynasty, British Museum, London/ Michael Holford, R. **47** *Statuette of Taweret*, British Museum, London/ Michael Holford, T; *Wall Painting from Tomb of Rekhmire, Thebes*/ Giraudon, B. **48** Illustration by Kate Simunek, T; *Chair of Hetepheres from Giza*, 4th Dynasty, Egyptian Museum, Cairo/ Robert Harding Picture Library, BL; *Painted Chest from Tomb of Kha*, 18th Dynasty, BR. **49** Illustration by Kate Simunek **50-51** Illustrations by Kate Simunek. **51** *Vase*, Pre-Dynasty, Fitzwilliam Museum, University of Cambridge/ The Bridgeman Art Library, B. **52-53** Illustration by Terence Dalley. **54** *Linen and Wool Tunic*, Louvre, Paris/ The Bridgeman Art Library, T; *Wall Painting from tomb of Ipy, Thebes*, 19th Dynasty, B. **55** *Wooden Statuette of Nobleman*, British Museum, London/ Michael Holford, L; *Wall Painting, Thebes*, 19th Dynasty, Louvre, Paris/ Giraudon, T; Illustration by Kate Simunek, BR. **56** *Relief from Tomb of Ramose, Thebes*, 18th Dynasty,/ Robert Harding Picture Library, T; *Bronze Mirror*, British Museum, London/ Michael Holford, B. **57** *Wall Painting from Tomb of Nakht, Thebes*, 18th Dynasty/ Giraudon. **58** *Queen Merit Amun from Deir el Bahari, Thebes*, 18th Dynasty, Egyptian Museum, Cairo/ E.T. Archive. **59** *Relief of Queen Kawit, Deir el Bahari, Thebes*, 11th Dynasty / Photography Jürgen Liepe, T; *Cosmetic Box*, British Museum, London MR. **60** *Wood and Ivory Cosmetic Spoon*, 18th Dynasty, Louvre, Paris/ Lauros-Giraudon. **61** *Glazed Beaded Necklace*, 18th Dynasty, British Museum, London/ Michael Holford, T; Pendant, Fitzwilliam Museum, University of Cambridge/ The Bridgeman Art Library, M; *Wall Painting of Queen Nefertari, Valley of the Queens*, 19th Dynasty/ Hirmer Archiv, MR; *Scarab Pectoral from Tomb of Tutankhamun, Thebes*, 18th Dynasty, Egyptian Museum, Cairo/ Giraudon/The Bridgeman Art Library, BL. **62** *Funerary Model*, 12th Dynasty, Fitzwilliam Museum, University of Cambridge/ The Bridgeman Art Library. **63** *Statuette from Thebes*, 18th Dynasty, Egyptian Museum, Cairo/ AGK, Berlin/ Photography Eric Lessing. **64** *Wall Painting from Tomb of Userhat, Sheik Abd el-Qurna, Thebes*, 19th Dynasty/ Werner Forman Archive. **65** *Wall Painting from Tomb of Nakht, Thebes*, 18th Dynasty, Giraudon, T; *Sarcophagus of Queen Kawit, Thebes*, from 11th Dynasty, Egyptian Museum, Cairo/ Photography Jürgen Liepe, B. **66** *Wall Painting from Tomb of Ipy*, Egyptian Museum, Turin/ Werner Forman Archive, T; *Wooden Statuette*, Middle Kingdom, Egyptian Museum, Berlin/ Wermer Forman Archive, M; *Wall Painting from Tomb of Nebamun*, 18th Dynasty, British Museum, London/ AGK, Berlin, B. **67** *Relief from Mastaba of Sopduhotep, Saqqara*, 5th Dynasty, Egyptian Museum, Berlin, (Bodemuseum)/ Werner Forman Archive, T; *Painted Ostracon*, British Museum, London, B. **68** *Relief from Tomb of Kagemni, Saqqara*/ Robert Harding Picture library. **69** *Scribes, Bas Relief from Tomb of Horemheb, Saqqara*, 18th Dynasty, Florence Archaeological Museum/ Giraudon. **70** *Funerary Model*, Egyptian Museum, Cairo/ Giraudon. **71, 72-73** Illustrations by Gill Tomblin. **72** Illustration by Kate Simunek, B. **74** *Wall Painting*, 18th Dynasty, Egyptian Museum, Cairo/ Scala. **75** *Relief of Akhenaten and family from Amarna*, 18th Dynasty, Egyptian Museum, Cairo/ AGK, Berlin. **76-77** Illustration by Terence Dalley. **78** *Head of Nefertiti*, Egyptian Museum, Berlin, (Bodemuseum) (MB 1243)/ Artephot/ Babey. **79** *Basalt Palette and Grinder, from Thebes*, 18th Dynasty, British Museum, London, TL; *A Painter's brushes and palette*, 18th Dynasty, Egyptian Museum, Cairo/ Giraudon, TR; Illustration by Gill Tomblin, B. **80** *Wall Painting*, 19th Dynasty, Egyptian Museum, Berlin, (Bodemuseum)/ Werner Forman Archive, BL; *Fragment of Relief*, 18th Dynasty, El-Minya Museum, Egypt/ Werner Forman Archive, BR. **81** *Relief from Tomb of Mereruka, Saqqara*, 6th Dynasty/ Werner Forman Archive, T; *Wall Painting from Tomb of Rekhmire, Thebes*, 18th Dynasty/ AGK, Berlin, M; *Funerary Model*, Egyptian Museum, Cairo/ Giraudon, B. **82** *Relief from Tomb of Mereruka, Saqqara*, 6th Dynasty/ Werner Forman Archive, TL; *Bracelet of Queen Ahhotep*, 18th Dynasty, Egyptian Museum, Cairo/ Artephot/ Photography Henri Stierlin, ML; *Pendant from Tomb of Tutankhamun*, 18th Dynasty, Egyptian Museum, Cairo/ Giraudon, MR. **83** *Map of Goldmines*, 20th Dynasty, Egyptian Museum, Turin/ Werner Forman Archive, T; *Wall Painting*, 18th Dynasty, British Museum, London, B. **84** *Wooden Statue of Ka-aper from Saqqara*, 5th Dynasty, Egyptian Museum, Cairo/ Werner Forman Archive, T; Illustration by Gill Tomblin, B. **85** *Wall Painting from Tomb of Menna, Thebes*, 18th Dynasty/ AGK, Berlin/ Photography Eric Lessing. **86-87** *Painted Box from Tomb of Tutankhamun*, 18th Dynasty, Egyptian Museum, Cairo/ Giraudon, T. *Painted Relief from Temple of Hatshepsut, Deir el-Bahari, Thebes*, 18th Dynasty / Michael Holford, BL: Illustration by Kate Simunek, BR. **89** *Funerary Model from Tomb of Mesehti*, 11th Dynasty, Egyptian Museum, Cairo/ Artephot. **90** *Statuette of Scribe from Saqqara*, 5th Dynasty, Egyptian Museum, Cairo/ Giraudon. **91** *Wall Painting from Tomb of Menna, Thebes*, 18th Dynasty/ Michael Holford. **92** *Wall Painting from Deir el-Medina*, 18th Dynasty / AGK, Berlin/ Photography Eric Lessing, BL; *Wall Painting from Tomb of Menna, Thebes*, 18th Dynasty / AGK, Berlin/ Photography Eric Lessing, BR. **93** Illustration by Gill Tomblin. **94** *Wall Painting*, Egyptian Museum, Berlin/ Scala, TL; *Wall Painting from Tomb of Khnumhotep, Beni Hassan*, 12th Dynasty, British Museum, London/ The Bridgeman Art Library, TR. **95, 96** Illustrations by Gill Tomblin. **97** *Wall Painting from Tomb of Menna, Thebes*, 18th Dynasty/ Michael Holford, TL; *Wall Painting from Tomb of Menna, Thebes*, 18th Dynasty, AGK, Berlin/ Photography Eric Lessing, TR. **98** *Wall Painting from Tomb of Sennefer, Thebes*, 18th Dynasty/ AGK, Berlin/ Photography Eric Lessing. **99** *Wall Paintings from Tomb of Menna*, 18th Dynasty/ Artephot/ Held, TL, MR; *Relief from Sarcophagus of Queen Ashayt, Thebes*, 11th Dynasty, Egyptian Museum, Cairo,(JE 47267)/ Photography Jürgen Liepe, BL. **100** *Relief from Tomb of Ti, Saqqara*, 6th Dynasty, T; *Funerary Model from Tomb of Meketre, Thebes*, 11th Dynasty, Egyptian Museum, Cairo/ Artephot/ Photography Babey, B. **101** Illustration by Gill Tomblin. **102** *Funerary Papyrus of the Royal Scribe Ani*, 19th Dynasty, British Museum, London (no: 10470), T; *Statue of Apis*, 30th Dynasty, British Museum, London/ Michael Holford, B; **103** *Statue of Sebek*, Ptolomaic Period, British Museum, London/ Michael Holford, T; Illustration by Gill Tomblin. **104** *Funerary Papyrus of the Royal Scribe Ani*, 19th Dynasty, British Museum, London (no: 10470/ 27), Michael Holford, T; *Limestone Ostracon*, New Kingdom, Louvre, Paris/ The Bridgeman Art Library, M. **105** *Gold and Enamel Hook belonging to Senusret II from Lahun*, 12th Dynasty/ E.T.Archive, T; *Funerary Papyrus of Royal Scribe, Ani*, 19th Dynasty, British Museum, London (no: 10470/ 27), B. **106** *Wall Painting*, Egyptian Museum, Cairo/ Artephot/ Held,T; *Wall Painting from Amarna*, Egyptian Museum, Cairo/ Robert Harding Picture Library/ Photography John Ross, M; *Figurine of Hippopotamus in Faience*, 12th Dynasty, Egyptian Museum, Berlin, (Charlottenburg) (no 13890)/ BPK, Berlin/ Photography M.Büsing, B. **107** *Wall Painting from Tomb of Nebamun, Thebes*, 18th Dynasty, British Museum, London/ E.T. Archive. **108** *Faience Dish*, 20th Dynasty, National Museum of Antiquities, Leiden/ Werner Forman Archive, T; **108-109** *Wall Painting from Tomb of Nebamun, Thebes*, 18th Dynasty/ The Bridgeman Art Library, B. **109** *Fragment from Wall Painting*, 17th Dynasty, Egyptian Museum, Turin/ AGK, Berlin/ Photography Eric Lessing, T. **110** Illustration by Gill Tomblin. **111** *Painted relief from Amarna*, 18th Dynasty, Egyptian Museum, Berlin, (Bodemuseum) (No. 14122)/ BPK, Berlin/ Photography Jürgen Liepe. **112** *Wall Painting from Tomb of Rekhmire*, 18th Dynasty / AGK, Berlin/ Photography Eric Lessing, T; *Harp from Thebes*, British Museum, London (EA 24564), B. **113** *Board Game*, Fitzwilliam Museum, University of Cambridge/ The Bridgeman Art Library. **114** *Funerary Papyrus of the Royal Scribe Hunefer*, 19th Dynasty, British Museum, London, (9901/ 5), T; *Gaming Board from Tomb of Tutankhamun*, 18th Dynasty, Egyptian Museum, Cairo, (JE 62058)/ Robert Harding Picture Library, B. **115** *Wall Painting from Deir el-Medina, Thebes*, 19th Dynasty, Egyptian Museum, Berlin, (Bodemuseum) (no. 21443)/ BPK, Berlin. **116** *Fly-Whisk from Tomb of Tutankhamun*, 18th Dynasty, Egyptian Museum, Cairo/ Robert Harding Picture Library/ Photography F.L. Kenett. **117** Illustration by Gill Tomblin. **118** *Tomb Relief*/ Giraudon. **119** *Funerary Papyrus of the Royal Scribe Hunefer*, 19th Dynasty, British Museum, London, (no: 9901/ 5). **120-121** *Funerary Papyrus of the Royal Scribe Ani*, 19th Dynasty, British Museum, London (no: 10470/ 18), B. **121** *Relief from Saqqara*, 19th Dynasty, Egyptian Museum, Cairo, (JE 4872)/ Photography Jorgen Liepe, T. **122** *Painted Shabti Box*, Louvre, Paris/ AGK, Berlin. **123** *Wall Painting from Tomb of Amun-nakht*, 19th Dynasty/ Photography Dr. Abdel-Ghaffar Shedid. **124** *Silver Figurine*, 19th Dynasty, Louvre, Paris/ The Bridgeman Art Library, **125** *Sarcophagus*, Museo Gregoriano Egizio, Vatican, Scala, T; *Mummified crocodile from Thebes*, Egyptian Museum, Cairo, (CG 29712) / Photography Jürgen Liepe, B. **126-127** Illustrations by Kate Simunek. **129, 130** Illustrations by Gill Tomblin. **131** *Statue of Khonsu-meh*, 21-22nd Dynasty, Egyptian Museum, Berlin, (no. 23732)/ BPK, Berlin, T; *Sistrum*, Graeco-Roman, Egyptian Museum, Cairo, (JE 53327)/ Photography Jürgen Liepe, B. **132-133** *Wall Paintings from Tomb of Sennefer, Thebes*, 18th Dynasty / AGK, Berlin/ Photography Eric Lessing. **134** *Sphinx and Pyramid, Giza*/ Magnum Photos/ Photography Richard Kalvar. **135** *Stela of the Workman Nefersenut*, British Museum, London. **136-137** Illustration by Terence Dalley. **138** *Limestone Ostracon*, Fitzwilliam Museum, University of Cambridge, (EGA. 43249-1943). **139** *Inner Coffin from Tomb of Tutankhamun*, Egyptian Museum, Cairo/ Photography Jürgen Liepe. **140** Illustration by Gill Tomblin. **141** *Canopic Jars*, Egyptian Museum, Balin, (no. 7185, 7187, 7184)/ AGK, Berlin/ Photography Eric Lessing, T; *Selkit from Tomb of Tutankhamun*, 18th Dynasty, (JE 60686)/ Photography Jürgen Liepe, B. **142** *Scribe's Chest*, New Kingdom, Louvre, Paris/ The Bridgeman Art Library. **143** *Relief from Tomb of Hesire, Saqqara*, 3rd Dynasty, Egyptian Museum, Cairo/ Werner Forman Archive, TR; *Statuette of Scribe from Amarna*, 18th Dynasty, Egyptian Museum, Berlin (INV. 22621) (Charlottenburg)/ BPK, Berlin, BL. **144** Illustration by Kate Simunek. **145** *Wall Painting from Tomb of Amenhirkhopshef, Valley of the Queens*, 20th Dynasty/ G. Dagli Orti, T; *Censer*, Museo Gregoriano Egizio, Vatican/ Scala, B. **146** Illustration by Gill Tomblin. **147** *Funerary Stele of Remi*, 18th Dynasty/ NY Carlsberg Glyptotek, Copenhagen, TR; *Statue with magical texts for healing*, 30th Dynasty, Louvre, Paris/ The Bridgeman Art Library, B. **148** *Relief from Temple of Kombo*, Roman Period / Carole Reeves. **149** *Painted Relief from Saqqara*/ Giraudon. **150** *Narmer's Palette*, Dynasty O, Egyptian Museum, Cairo, (JE 32169)/ Photography Jürgen Liepe, TL; *Head of Userkaf*, Egyptian Museum, Cairo, 5th Dynasty, (JE 90220)/ Photography Jürgen Liepe, TR; *Funerary Model from Thebes*, 12th Dynasty, Egyptian Museum, Berlin, (ÄM 12) (Charlottenburg)/ BPK, Berlin/ Photography M. Büsing, ML; *Wall Painting from Tomb of Menna, Thebes*, 18th Dynasty/ Werner Forman Archive, MR; *Detail from the Standard of Ur, Sumerian*, c. 2600 BC, British Museum, London/ Michael Holford, B. **151** *Decorative Tile from a Ramesside palace, Tell el-Yahudiya*, 20th Dynasty, British Museum, London, (EA 12337), TL; *Head of Senusret from Thebes*, 12th Dynasty, Egyptian Museum, Berlin, (INV. 9529)/ BPK, Berlin/ Photography Jürgen Liepe, TR; *Statuette of Osiris*, Egyptian Museum, Berlin (INV 905), (Bodemuseum)/ BPK, Berlin/ Photography Jürgen Liepe, ML; *Satirical Papyrus from Thebes*, Late New Kingdom, British Museum, London, (EA 10016). *Stele of Hammnrabi*, 1700 BC, Louvre, Paris/ Michael Holford, BL; *Sumerian Cuneiform Tablet from Warka*, c. 2100 BC, British Museum London/ Michael Holford, BR. **152** *Ceremonial Axe of Ahmose*, 18th Dynasty, Egyptian Museum, Cairo/ Photography Jürgen Liepe, TL; *Wall Painting from Tomb of Nebamun, Thebes*, 18th Dynasty, British Museum, London, (EA 37982), MR; *Gold Mask from the Acropolis of Mycenae*, 16th Century BC, National Archaeological Museum, Athens/ The Bridgeman Art Library, ML; *Bronze Chinese Ritual Vessel*, Shang Period, Musee Cernuschi, Paris/ Michael Holford, BL; *The Dolphin Fresco, Minoan, from Knossos, Crete*, c 1450-1400 BC/ Michael Holford, BR. **153** *Relief from Tomb of Horemheb*, 18th Dynasty, Archaeological Museum, Bologna/ Scala, TL; *Painted Ostracon from Deir el-Medina*, 19th Dynasty, Louvre, Paris/ Lauros-Giraudon, M; *Detail from bronze bands on the gates from the Temple of Mamu*, 858-824 BC, British Museum, London/ Michael Holford, B. **154** *Figure of King Pimay*, 22nd Dynasty, British Museum, London, (EA 32747), TR; *Statuette of Bastet*, 26th Dynasty, Egyptian Museum, Cairo/ Photography Jürgen Liepe, ML; *Woman Wearing Egyptian Wig, Phoenician Ivory*, 9-8th century BC, British Museum, London/ Michael Holford, MR; *Etruscan Sarcophagus from Cerreteri*, Museo di Villa Giulia, Rome/ Toucan Books Archive, B. **155** *Head of Nectanebo*, 30th Dynasty, Egyptian Museum, Munich, TR; *Limestone Ostracon from Thebes*, New Kingdom, British Museum, London, MR; *Greek coin of electrum, from Ephesus*, British Museum, London, BL; *Bronze Statuette of Alexander the Great*, Roman Imperial Period, British Museum, London/ Michael Holford, B.

Front Cover : Illustration by Kate Simunek, T; British Museum, London, M; Egyptian Museum, Cairo/ Giraudon/The Bridgeman Art Library, London, MR; Magnum Photos/Photography Richard Kalvar, BM; Egyptian Museum, Berlin (Charlottenburg), BPK/Photography M. Büsing, BR.
Back Cover: Louvre, Paris/The Bridgeman Art Library, London, T; Egyptian Museum, Berlin (odesmuseum) BPK/Photography Jürgen Liepe. ML; AKG, Berlin/Photography Eric Lessing, M; Egyptian Museum, Cairo/Robert Harding Picture Library/Photography F. L. Kenett, B.

Toucan Books thank the following for their kind permission to quote passages from the publications below:
Ashmolean Museum from *Ancient Egypt* by P.R.S. Morey 1992.
British Museum Press from *The Ancient Egyptian Book of the Dead* by R.O. Faulkner 1985; *Egyptian Life* by Miriam Stead 1986; *Egyptian Myths* by George Hart 1990; *Voices from Ancient Egypt* by R.B. Parkinson 1991; *The Cat in Ancient Egypt* by Jaromir Malek 1993; *Women in Ancient Egypt* by Gay Robins 1993.
Cambridge University Press from *Life in Ancient Egypt* by Eugen Strouhal 1992.
Dover Publications from *Life in Ancient Egypt* by Adolf Erman 1971.
Michael Joseph from *People of the Nile* by John Romer 1989.
Penguin Books Limited: Penguin Classics edition from Herodotus, *The Histories*, Book 2.
Rubicon Press from *Growing Up in Ancient Egypt* by Rosalind M and Jac. J. Janssen 1990.
Shire Publications from *Egyptian Food and Drink* by Hilary Wilson 1988.
Thames and Hudson from *The Egyptians* by Cyril Aldred 1961.
Time Life Inc Books from *Ancient Egypt* by Lionel Casson 1969; *Egypt: Land of the Pharaohs* (Lost Civilizations).

59-010-4